I want to be a
CHEF

I want to be a CHEF

MURDOCH BOOKS

contents

let's cook...

Learning to cook is an investment for life. That may sound serious, but cooking is actually one of the most fun things you can do. Not only will it give you a sense of achievement to know how to cook great meals, snacks and treats, it will give your friends and family a lot of pleasure, too. With this book to help you, you'll soon be cooking just like a professional.

How to start

To be a successful cook, you must be organised. A professional chef relies on a well-run, tidy kitchen in order to create a large number of meals in a short time. You need to work in the same way, even if you have plenty of time and are only cooking for yourself. Working in a messy kitchen is no fun and doesn't produce great results. There are other important things you need to know, too.

◆ Read all the way through the recipe and carefully check the list of ingredients to make sure you have everything you need before you start. Having to run to the shops in the middle of cooking is not a good idea.

◆ Make sure you have the right equipment. Put the kitchen scales on the bench. Have the electric whisk ready, and so on.

◆ Prepare any baking tins or moulds. They may have to be greased with oil or butter, or lined with baking paper.

◆ Before you start to cook, prepare all the ingredients you can. Open tins, peel and chop vegetables, grate cheese and measure flour, sugar and butter. Otherwise, you'll be stopping and starting all the time, which can be time consuming. And, it can create lots of mess. Be sure to clean up as you go.

◆ Read the recipe as you go and check that you're adding ingredients in the right order.

◆ Preheat the oven. If you put things in the oven and then switch it on to cook the food, the food will dry out, and it won't be cooked when the recipe says it should. See more information about oven use on the next page.

◆ Be sure to have a kitchen timer or clock handy, to keep track of cooking times.

How to weigh and measure

When you have been cooking for a while, you'll be able to estimate quantities fairly accurately, but until then, it's important that you measure carefully, especially when baking a cake or making cookies.

You'll see that there are three different scales for measuring: metric, imperial and cup measures. So, there should be something to suit every kitchen. A cup measure is a standard 250 ml (9 fl oz). Whichever scale you use, you must stay with it throughout a recipe and not chop and change.

You will need:
◆ a set of dry measuring cups, usually in a set of four: a 250 ml (9fl oz/1 cup) measure, a 125 ml (4 fl oz/½ cup), 80 ml (2½ fl oz/⅓ cup) and 60 ml (2 fl oz/¼ cup) measure. These are used for ingredients such as flour and sugar.

◆ a liquid measuring cup with a lip. This should have lines on the side that clearly show the measures.

◆ a set of measuring spoons for 1 tablespoon, 1 teaspoon, ½ teaspoon and ¼ teaspoon. You can buy metal or colourful plastic ones.

Liquid measures

Place the liquid measuring cup on the bench, then add some of the liquid and bend down so your eyes are level with the measurement marks. Check if you have too much or too little liquid and add or remove, as necessary.

Dry measures

Spoon dry ingredients into the measuring cup or spoon and then level them off with a knife or metal spatula. Cup and spoon measures for dry ingredients should be level, not heaped (unless the recipe specifically says otherwise).

How to use the oven

If you're using the oven, place the shelves at the correct height before you turn it on. Always preheat the oven before putting things in to cook. Most of them have a light to show when the right temperature has been reached.

If you have a fan-forced oven (ask an adult, if you're not sure), the temperature will be a bit hotter than a normal oven. The temperatures given in the recipes in this book are for a normal oven. If you use a fan-forced oven, you don't need to worry about preheating it, but you will need to reduce the temperature for each recipe by about 10°C (18°F). This is most important

Chopping boards

When you have chopped raw meat, chicken or seafood on a board, you must scrub the board and the knife in very hot water with detergent before using them for any other ingredients. Ask an adult to help; you must take care not to scald your hands. Ideally, have two boards: one for raw meat, chicken and fish, and one for fruit and vegetables.

for baking cakes, slices and cookies and other sweet things. It is less important for things such as roasts.

How to serve your cooking

If you like watching cooking programs on the television, you'll know that most chefs arrange the different items of food on the plate in an attractive way. While you don't need to spend a lot of time doing this (hot food will go cold if you fiddle around too long), it does add to the pleasure of eating if the food is arranged neatly and not just plopped on in a messy way. After all the trouble you've taken to cook the dish well, it makes sense to 'plate' it properly. While your food is cooking, set the table with all the plates, cutlery and glassware you like; the more attractive the setting, the more everyone will enjoy your efforts.

Food safety

Knowing how to store and transport food safely is very important. You don't want all your hard work in the kitchen to go to waste because food has spoiled. Spoiled food can make you ill.

How to handle uncooked meat

◆ As a general rule, raw meat will keep for up to 3 days in the fridge and up to 6 months in the freezer.

◆ To freeze meat, wrap each piece in plastic wrap, then put it in a freezer bag. Make sure that you get all the air out of the bag. Ask an adult if you need help. Label and date the bag because, once something is frozen, it is very hard to recognise what it is.

◆ To thaw, put it on a large plate and leave in the fridge. Allow enough time for it to defrost fully before starting to cook. If you're not sure, ask an adult, Depending on the size of the item, it can take several hours or may need leaving overnight. Never thaw meat at room temperature or under water. Do not re-freeze thawed meat unless you cook it first.

How to handle uncooked chicken

Chicken should be treated very carefully as it can harbour dangerous bacteria.

◆ Keep it in the fridge for 2 days at the most, and up to 6 months in the freezer.

◆ Thaw chicken in the same way as meat. Cook it within 12 hours of thawing. Never let raw chicken (or other raw meat) come in contact with other foods in the fridge.

How to handle cooked food

◆ Cool hot food quickly that you need to store. Put it in the fridge as soon as steam has stopped rising.

◆ Make sure that food is completely cooked through. This is particularly important for chicken and minced meat.

◆ When you're reheating food, make sure it's steaming hot before you serve it and isn't hot on the outside and still cold in the middle. If you're using a microwave, make sure you stir the food while reheating.

Food allergies

You may know someone who has an allergy to a particular food and must avoid it or they could become very ill. If you're having friends round for something to eat, ask an adult in the family to find out if any of them has a food intolerance, so you don't prepare something they cannot eat. If someone has a severe nut allergy (peanuts, cashews and so on), make sure there are no foods containing even the tiniest amount. Don't serve nuts or small sweets to children under five as they could choke on them.

◆ If you're packing food in a lunchbox, use one that's insulated or comes with a freezer pack. Don't pack hot foods in your lunchbox. First let them cool in the fridge overnight.

Hygiene and personal safety

1 Always ask an adult for permission before you start to cook. And always ask for help if you are not confident with chopping or handling hot cake tins.

2 Before you start, wash your hands well with soap and water, tie back long hair and wear an apron to protect your clothes. Have oven gloves and tea towels handy.

3 When you're cooking on the stovetop, turn pan handles to the side so there's no danger of knocking them as you walk past. When stirring, hold the pan handle firmly.

4 Never use electrical appliances near water. Always have dry hands before you touch any appliance. Once you've finished using an appliance, switch it off at the power point and remove the plug from the wall before cleaning it.

5 Always use thick, dry oven gloves when you're getting things out of the oven.

6 Remember to turn off the oven, hotplate or gas ring when you have finished using it.

7 Wash up regularly as you go along. This will save hours of cleaning at the end and will keep your workspace clear.

Baking tips

Making cakes and cookies requires some special techniques and ways of working.

◆ As usual, first read the recipe. Take any chilled ingredients such as butter and eggs from the fridge and set aside on the kitchen bench to reach room temperature. If you need to beat butter, you won't be able to work with it if it's a hard, solid lump.

◆ Line the tin(s) with baking paper, following the recipe instructions, or butter and dust lightly with flour. Always use the shape and size of tin specified in the recipe, because it affects the cooking time.

◆ Before you turn on the oven, position the shelf in the centre of the oven, making sure there is enough room above it for the cake to rise. Preheat the oven to the temperature stated in the recipe.

◆ Weigh and measure all the ingredients properly before you start.

◆ Add eggs or egg yolks to a cake mixture one at a time, beating well after you add each egg. Don't put them all in together.

◆ To whisk egg whites, make sure the bowl and beaters (or whisk) are clean and dry. Just a hint of grease, and the egg whites won't whisk properly.

◆ Dry ingredients should always be folded into a whisked egg and sugar mixture with a large metal spoon. Fold gently from the centre of the bowl outwards. Fold whisked egg whites into the other ingredients (not the other way round).

◆ Spoon thick cake batters into the prepared tin and pour in thinner batters. Smooth the surface of the batter with a spatula or the back of a spoon because, if it looks like the surface of the Moon, it won't cook or brown evenly.

Cooking for a healthy life

Healthy eating is important throughout your life and it's a good idea to know how food works in your body. There are five food groups: protein, carbohydrate, fibre, fat and vitamins and minerals, all of which play different roles.

Remove toothpicks from food before serving to children under five.

◆ Proteins, such as meat, fish, dairy (cheese, milk and eggs), pulses and nuts, will build your muscles and help you grow. Protein also takes longer to digest, so can keep you feeling full for longer and prevent snacking.

◆ Carbohydrates, such as bread, potatoes, rice and pasta, give you energy.

◆ Fibre keeps your insides working properly.

◆ Fat is important, in small amounts, especially for bodies that are still growing. Fats from oily fish, seeds, nuts, avocado and olive oil are the best fats to include regularly.

◆ Vitamins come from eating plenty of fruit and vegetables.

If you have a sensible, balanced diet, eating the occasional sweet treat is not going to do you any harm. All things in moderation.

And, finally...have fun cooking and enjoy your journey to becoming a top-notch chef

How to use this book

All the recipes are broken down into a few simple steps. They all have photographs so you can see what your finished dish is going to look like. Don't worry too much if it doesn't look exactly the same…the taste is what matters. Some recipes have step-by-step photographs, too, to help you with any techniques you may not know or are finding difficult to do.

start the day

blueberry pancakes

MAKES 12

250 g (9 oz/2 cups) plain (all-purpose) flour

2 teaspoons baking powder

1 teaspoon bicarbonate of soda
(baking soda)

75 g (2½ oz/⅓ cup) sugar

2 eggs

80 g (2¾ oz) unsalted butter, melted

310 ml (10¾ fl oz/1¼ cups) milk

310 g (11 oz/2 cups) blueberries,
fresh or frozen

honey and plain yoghurt, to serve (optional)

1 Sift the flour, baking powder and bicarbonate of soda into a large bowl. Add the sugar and make a well in the centre. Add the eggs, melted butter and milk to the dry ingredients, stirring just to combine (add more milk if you prefer a thinner batter).

2 Gently fold the blueberries into the batter (leave some for serving). Heat a frying pan and brush lightly with melted butter or oil. Drop tablespoons of batter into the pan and cook over low heat until bubbles appear and pop on the surface.

3 Turn the pancakes over and cook the other side (these pancakes can be difficult to handle so take care when turning). Transfer to a plate and cover with a cloth to keep warm while you cook the rest of the batter. Serve warm with some blueberries, a drizzle of honey and plain yoghurt, if using.

french toast

SERVES 2

2 eggs

250 ml (9 fl oz/1 cup) milk

1/2 teaspoon vanilla extract

40 g (1 1/2 oz) butter

4 thick slices day-old bread

ground cinnamon and sugar, to serve

1 Break the eggs into a wide shallow dish and add the milk and vanilla extract. Beat with a fork or wire whisk until well mixed.

2 Melt half the butter in a frying pan. When the butter begins to bubble, quickly dip a piece of bread into the egg mixture, let the excess run off, then place it in the pan.

3 Cook for 1–2 minutes. When it is golden underneath, turn the bread over and cook the other side.

4 Transfer the French toast to a plate and cover with foil to keep warm while you cook the rest. Add more butter to the pan as needed and cook the remaining bread. Serve sprinkled with cinnamon and sugar.

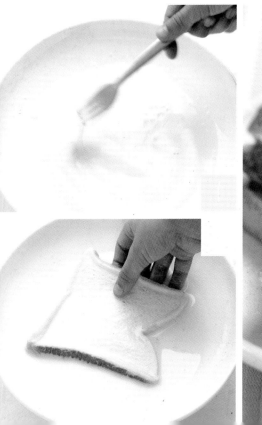

scrambled eggs

SERVES 2

4 eggs

3 tablespoons milk

15 g (¹/₂ oz) butter

toast or English muffins, to serve

1 Beat the eggs and milk lightly with a fork.

2 Melt the butter in a heavy-based frying pan over very low heat and pour in the egg. Stir constantly with a wooden spoon, lifting the mixture from the bottom of the pan so that it cooks evenly. The eggs are ready when they are just set but are still creamy.

3 Remove from the heat and serve immediately on toast or English muffins.

ham and corn muffins

MAKES 24

125 g (4¹/₂ oz/1 cup) self-raising flour

40 g (1¹/₂ oz) ham, chopped

60 g (2¹/₄ oz/¹/₃ cup) tinned corn kernels, drained

¹/₄ red capsicum (pepper), deseeded and finely chopped

2 teapoons chopped flat-leaf (Italian) parsley

60 g (2¹/₄ oz) unsalted butter, melted

125 ml (4 fl oz/¹/₂ cup) milk

1 egg

1 tablespoon sesame seeds

1. Preheat the oven to 210°C (415°F/Gas 6–7). Brush 24 mini muffin holes with oil. Sift the flour into a large bowl. Add the ham, corn, capsicum and parsley and stir to combine.

2. Mix the melted butter, milk and egg in a bowl. Make a well in the centre of the flour mixture and add the milk mixture. Mix the dough lightly until the ingredients are just combined.

3. Spoon the mixture into the muffin holes and sprinkle with the sesame seeds. Bake for 15–20 minutes, or until golden.

berry muffins

MAKES 16

250 g (9 oz/1 cup) plain yoghurt

100 g (3¹/₂ oz/1 cup) rolled (porridge) oats

3 tablespoons oil

80 g (2³/₄ oz/¹/₃ cup) caster (superfine) sugar

1 egg

125 g (4¹/₂ oz/1 cup) self-raising flour, sifted

3 teaspoons baking powder

200 g (7 oz/1¹/₃ cups) frozen mixed berries, thawed

1. Preheat the oven to 180°C (350°F/Gas 4). Place paper cases into 16 standard muffin holes. Mix the yoghurt, oats, oil, caster sugar and egg in a bowl. Gently stir in the sifted flour and baking powder with the berries.

2. Spoon the mixture into the paper cases. Bake for 20–25 minutes, or until the muffins are golden brown.

toast toppers

2 slices bread

1/2 tomato, sliced

125 g (4 1/2 oz/1 cup) grated cheese

1/2 avocado, mashed

1 Top 1 slice of toast with the slices of tomato. Grill (broil) for about 1 minute. Sprinkle with half the grated cheese. Grill until the cheese melts. Slice into fingers.

2 Spread 1 slice of toast with the mashed avocado. Sprinkle with the remaining grated cheese and grill until the cheese melts. Slice into fingers.

Variations: Spread toast with mashed baked beans and sprinkle with grated cheese. Grill until the cheese melts.

Mix together 60 g (2 1/4 oz/1/2 cup) grated cheese and 1 slice of ham, finely chopped. Spread over a slice of toast and grill until the cheese melts.

Note: Toppings can also be put on crumpets and English muffins.

ricotta crumpets with pear

SERVES 1–2

2 crumpets

2 tablespoons ricotta cheese

1 pear, thinly sliced

2 teaspoons honey or maple syrup

1 tablespoon sultanas (golden raisins)

pinch ground cinnamon (optional)

1   Put the crumpets in a toaster. Toast until golden. Spread with the ricotta cheese.

2   Top the crumpets with slices of the pear. Drizzle with the honey. Sprinkle with the sultanas and cinnamon.

Note: For added fibre, use wholemeal (whole-wheat) crumpets.

multi-grain porridge

350 g (12 oz/4 cups) wholegrain rolled (porridge) oats

100 g (3½ oz/1 cup) rice flakes

120 g (4 oz/1 cup) rye flakes

200 g (7 oz/1 cup) millet

2 tablespoons sesame seeds, lightly toasted

2 teaspoons linseeds (flax seeds)

low-fat milk or plain yoghurt, to serve

soft brown sugar, to serve

1 Put the rolled oats, rice flakes, rye flakes, millet, sesame seeds and linseeds in a bowl and stir well. Store in an airtight container until needed.

2 To prepare the porridge for two people, put 125 g (4½ oz/1 cup) of the dry mixture, a pinch of salt and 250 ml (9 fl oz/1 cup) of water in a saucepan. Stir well, then set aside for 10 minutes (this creates a smoother, creamier porridge).

3 Stir again and then add another 250 ml (9 fl oz/1 cup) of water.

4 Bring to the boil over medium heat, stirring occasionally. Reduce the heat to low and simmer the porridge, stirring often, for 12–15 minutes, or until the mixture is soft and creamy.

5 Serve with milk or yoghurt and brown sugar.

layered cereal and apple yoghurt

125 g (4^1/$_2$ oz/^{1}/$_2$ cup) low-fat plain or fruit-flavoured yoghurt

^{1}/$_2$ red apple, unpeeled, finely grated

70 g (2^1/$_2$ oz/1 cup) crunchy breakfast cereal

^{1}/$_2$ teaspoon soft brown sugar or honey

1   Combine the yoghurt and apple in a small bowl.

2   Layer the cereal and yoghurt mixture in small, wide glasses.

3   Sprinkle the top with brown sugar or honey. Serve immediately.

Hint: You can use any type of cereal for this breakfast, such as natural muesli, but choose one that won't go soft too quickly when mixed with the yoghurt.

Note: This recipe is a great one for quick starts, as no cooking is needed.

dried fruit compote with yoghurt

SERVES 4

50 g (1³/₄ oz/¹/₃ cup) dried apricots, quartered

50 g (1³/₄ oz/¹/₄ cup) stoned prunes, quartered

50 g (1³/₄ oz/²/₃ cup) dried pears, chopped

50 g (1³/₄ oz/²/₃ cup) dried peaches, chopped

185 ml (6 fl oz/³/₄ cup) orange juice

1 cinnamon stick

plain yoghurt, to serve

1. Put the fruit, orange juice and cinnamon stick in a saucepan over medium heat and stir to combine.

2. Bring to the boil, then reduce the heat to low, cover, and simmer for 10 minutes, or until the fruit is plump and softened.

3. Discard the cinnamon stick. Serve drizzled with the cooking liquid and a dollop of the plain yoghurt.

Note: This fruity breakfast is full of flavour and is a great source of fibre, calcium and potassium with small but important amounts of iron and beta-carotene.

Storage: Store in an airtight container in the refrigerator for up to 1 week.

fruit kebabs with honey yoghurt

MAKES 4

4 strawberries, hulled

1 banana, chopped

1 kiwi fruit, peeled and chopped

¹/₄ small pineapple, peeled and chopped

¹/₄ rockmelon (netted melon/canteloupe), seeded and chopped

200 g (7 oz) plain yoghurt

2 tablespoons honey

1. Thread the pieces of fruit onto 4 iceblock (popsicle/ ice lolly) sticks.

2. Combine the yoghurt and honey in a bowl. Serve as a dipping sauce for the fruit.

summer fruity yoghurt

SERVES 4

2 ripe pears, unpeeled

2 teaspoon lemon juice

80 g (2¾ oz/½ cup) fresh or frozen
blueberries

125 g (4½ oz) strawberries, hulled, halved
and quartered

100 g (3½ oz) raspberries

pulp of 2 passionfruit

1 tablespoon caster (superfine) sugar

500 g (1 lb 2 oz/2 cups) low-fat vanilla or
fruit-flavoured yoghurt

1. Remove the core from the pears. Cut into chunks and put into a large bowl. Sprinkle with the lemon juice.

2. Add the blueberries, strawberries, raspberries and passionfruit and sprinkle with the sugar. Set aside for 10 minutes to infuse.

3. Gently fold in the yoghurt.

4. Spoon into four glasses and chill for at least 20 minutes.

Hint: For variety you can also make this recipe with raspberries, nectarines or peaches, or chopped citrus fruits.

berry smoothie

SERVES 2

2 bananas, chopped

200 g (7 oz) mixed berries

3 tablespoons low-fat vanilla fromage frais or whipped yoghurt

500 ml (17 fl oz/2 cups) skim milk

1 tablespoon oat bran

1 Put the banana, berries, fromage frais, milk and oat bran in a blender or food processor.

2 Blend or process for 2 minutes, or until thick and creamy.

breakfast smoothie

SERVES 2

150 g (5$\frac{1}{2}$ oz) fresh low-GI fruit (such as peaches, plums, nectarines, apricots, pears, apples or any type of berry)

60 g (2$\frac{1}{4}$ oz/$\frac{1}{4}$ cup) low-fat vanilla yoghurt

250 ml (9 fl oz/1 cup) low-fat milk (or soy milk)

1 tablespoon malted milk powder

2 teaspoons wheat germ

1 Put the fruit, yoghurt, milk, milk powder and wheat germ in a blender or food processor.

2 Blend or process until well combined.

Hints: Experiment with various low-GI fruits to work out your favourite combination for this low-fat smoothie.

blueberry starter

SERVES 2

200 g (7 oz) blueberries

250 g (9 oz/1 cup) plain yoghurt

250 ml (9 fl oz/1 cup) milk

1 tablespoon wheat germ

1–2 teaspoons honey, to taste

1 Put the blueberries, yoghurt, milk, wheat germ and honey in a blender or food processor.

2 Blend or process until smooth.

wheaty starter

SERVES 2

2 breakfast wheat biscuits

2 bananas, chopped

60 g (2$\frac{1}{4}$ oz/$\frac{1}{4}$ cup) vanilla soy yoghurt

500 ml (17 fl oz/2 cups) low-fat soy milk

1 Put the wheat biscuits, banana, yoghurt and soy milk in a blender or food processor.

2 Blend or process until smooth.

lunchtime and snacks

bits and pieces with dip

tzatziki

2 Lebanese (short) cucumbers, deseeded and grated

185 g (6$^{1}/_{2}$ oz/$^{3}/_{4}$ cup) plain yoghurt

2 garlic cloves, crushed

1 teaspoon lemon juice

1 teaspoon chopped dill

$^{1}/_{4}$ teaspoon chopped mint

hummus

220 g (7$^{3}/_{4}$ oz/1 cup) dried chickpeas

4 tablespoons olive oil, plus extra to drizzle

3–4 tablespoons lemon juice

2 garlic cloves, crushed

2 tablespoons tahini

1 tablespoon ground cumin

avocado dip

$^{1}/_{2}$ avocado

30 g (1 oz/$^{1}/_{4}$ cup) grated cheddar cheese

$^{1}/_{4}$ tomato, chopped

cottage cheese, to serve (optional)

selection of sliced blanched vegetables (see Hint), to serve

small pieces of cheese, to serve

1 To make the tzatziki, mix the cucumber with the remaining ingredients and serve with the sliced vegetables. If you like, offer some poppadoms or chunks of bread.

2 To make the hummus, soak the chickpeas in water for 8 hours, or overnight. Drain. Put in a saucepan and cover with cold water. Bring to the boil and cook for 50–60 minutes. Drain, keeping 250 ml (9 fl oz/1 cup) of the cooking liquid. Put the chickpeas in a food processor with the oil, lemon juice, garlic, tahini and cumin. Blend well until the mixture starts to look thick and creamy. With the motor running, gradually add the cooking liquid until the mixture is as thick or thin as you like it. Transfer to a bowl and drizzle with olive oil.

3 To make the avocado dip, combine the avocado, cheese and tomato.

4 Arrange small pieces of cheese and vegetable sticks in a lunchbox or small container. Serve with the dips.

Hint: Choose your favourite vegetables or a selection which might include cauliflower, baby corn, broccoli, spring onion (scallion), beans, snow peas (mangetout), mushrooms, celery, zucchini (courgette), cucumber, capsicum (pepper), carrot and cherry tomatoes.

gluten-free bread rolls

MAKES 8 INDIVIDUAL LOAVES

canola oil, for greasing

15 g (1/2 oz) dried yeast (4 teaspoons)

1 tablespoon soft brown sugar

500 ml (17 fl oz/2 cups) warm water

2 teaspoons guar gum (from health food stores)

300 g (10 1/2 oz/2 cups) soy-free, gluten-free plain (all-purpose) flour

130 g (4 3/4 oz/3/4 cup) rice flour

2 teaspoons ground sea salt

45 g (1 1/2 oz/1/2 cup) rice bran

60 g (2 1/4 oz) dairy-free margarine, melted and cooled

canola oil, for brushing

1. Preheat the oven to 200°C (400°F/Gas 6). Lightly grease eight 10 x 5.5 x 3.5 cm (4 x 2 1/4 x 1 1/2 inch) individual loaf (bar) tins.

2. Combine the yeast, sugar and warm water in a bowl. Stand the bowl in a warm place for about 10 minutes, or until the mixture is frothy.

3. Sift the gum and flours into a large bowl. Add the salt and rice bran. Make a well in the centre and add the yeast mixture and cooled margarine.

4. Mix well to form a soft dough. Divide into eight portions, then shape each into an oval shape. Put in the prepared tins.

5. Cover and leave in a warm place for 45 minutes, or until the mixture comes to the top of the tins.

6. Bake for 25–30 minutes, or until cooked through. Remove from the tins and leave to cool on a wire rack.

carrot and zucchini muffins

MAKES 18

35 g (1¼ oz/¼ cup) wholemeal flour

30 g (1 oz/¼ cup) plain (all-purpose) flour

1 teaspoon baking powder

1 tablespoon soft brown sugar

½ small carrot, grated

¼ small zucchini (courgette), grated

½ tablespoon poppy seeds

30 g (1 oz) unsalted butter, melted

1 egg white, lightly beaten

2 tablespoons milk

1 Preheat the oven to 210°C (415°F/Gas 6–7). Line 18 mini muffin holes with patty cases.

2 Sift the flours and baking powder in a bowl. Add the brown sugar, carrot, zucchini and poppy seeds. Mix.

3 Combine the butter, egg white and milk. Add the milk mixture to the dry ingredients. Using a wooden spoon, stir until ingredients are just combined.

4 Divide the mixture evenly among the muffin holes. Bake for 20 minutes, or until golden.

5 Cool for 5 minutes, then turn out onto a wire rack to cool.

spinach and feta muffins

MAKES 20

90 g (3¼ oz) English spinach leaves

155 g (5½ oz) self-raising flour

¼ teaspoon paprika

60 g (2¼ oz) feta cheese, crumbled

2 spring onions (scallions), finely chopped

¼ tablespoon chopped fresh dill

125 ml (4 fl oz/½ cup) buttermilk

1 egg, lightly beaten

2 tablespoons olive oil

30 g (1 oz) feta cheese, crumbled, extra

1 Preheat the oven to 200°C (400°F/Gas 6). Lightly grease 20 mini muffin holes.

2 Steam the spinach until just tender. Drain and squeeze out any excess liquid. Chop finely.

3 Sift the flour and paprika into a bowl and stir in the feta, spring onion and dill. Make a well in the centre.

4 Combine the buttermilk, half the beaten egg mixture and the oil. Add the spinach and fold gently.

5 Divide the mixture evenly among the muffin holes. Sprinkle the feta over the top. Bake for 25 minutes, or until golden. Cool for 5 minutes, then turn out onto a wire rack to cool.

light chicken caesar salad

SERVES 2

2 thick slices wholemeal (whole-wheat) or wholegrain bread

oil spray

25 g (1 oz) bacon slices, thinly sliced

½ cos (romaine) lettuce, outer leaves and core removed

1 cooked chicken breast fillet, sliced

2 anchovy fillets, drained, rinsed and halved lengthways

15 g (½ oz) shredded parmesan cheese

1 tablespoon finely chopped flat-leaf (Italian) parsley

low-fat dressing

60 g (2¼ oz) low-fat plain yoghurt

1½ tablespoons low-fat mayonnaise dressing

2 teaspoons Dijon mustard

2 teaspoons lemon juice

¼ teaspoon Worcestershire sauce

1 Preheat the oven to 180°C (350°F/Gas 4). Remove the crusts from the bread and cut into 1 cm (½ inch) cubes. Place on a tray. Bake for 12 minutes, or until lightly browned.

2 Lightly spray a small frying pan with oil. Cook the bacon over medium heat for 2 minutes, or until cooked. Drain on paper towels.

3 Combine the dressing ingredients in a bowl.

4 Break the lettuce leaves into smaller pieces. Add the chicken, bread, bacon, half of the anchovies, and parmesan.

5 Toss through two-thirds of the dressing. Scatter over the remaining anchovies, parsley and parmesan. Drizzle over the remaining dressing.

Hint: You can use poached or barbecued chicken breast in this recipe. Remove any skin and fat.

creamy chicken and corn soup

SERVES 6

1 litre (35 fl oz/4 cups) salt-reduced chicken stock

40 g (1½ oz/½ cup) small pasta

175 g (6 oz/1 cup) finely chopped cooked chicken (see Hint)

125 g (4½ oz/½ cup) tinned creamed corn

1 tablespoon chopped flat-leaf (Italian) parsley

1 Put the stock and pasta in a saucepan. Bring to the boil, then reduce the heat and simmer for 10–12 minutes, or until tender.

2 Add the chicken and corn and simmer for 5 minutes.

3 Stir in the parsley and cool slightly. Process in a blender or food processor until smooth. Reheat to serve.

Hint: Use skinless barbecued (grilled) chicken or cooked chicken breast, sliced.

potato and pumpkin soup

SERVES 4

1 tablespoon canola oil

1 leek, halved lengthways, washed and sliced

2 garlic cloves, peeled and crushed

500 g (1 lb 2 oz) white-skinned potatoes, peeled and chopped

500 g (1 lb 2 oz) butternut pumpkin (squash), peeled, deseeded and chopped

1 litre (35 fl oz/4 cups) vegetable stock

finely chopped chives, to serve

sour cream, to serve (optional)

1 Heat the oil in a saucepan over medium heat. Add the leek and garlic and cook, stirring, for 2 minutes. Reduce the heat to low. Cover the pan with a lid and cook, stirring occasionally, for 8 minutes, or until the leek is very soft.

2 Add the potato, pumpkin and stock to the pan. Bring to the boil. Reduce the heat and simmer for about 20 minutes, or until the vegetables are very soft. Set aside to cool slightly.

3 Purée the soup in a blender or food processor until smooth. Reheat to serve.

minestrone

SERVES 4–6

2 tablespoons olive oil

1 onion, chopped

1 bacon slice, finely chopped

3 carrots, halved lengthways and chopped

3 zucchini (courgettes), halved lengthways and chopped

2 celery stalks, sliced

2 all-purpose potatoes, chopped

400 g (14 oz) tinned diced tomatoes

300 g (10½ oz/1½ cups) tinned four-bean mix, drained and rinsed

30 g (1 oz/⅓ cup) small pasta shapes

125 g (4½ oz/1 cup) green beans, trimmed and sliced

grated parmesan cheese, to serve

chopped flat-leaf (Italian) parsley, to serve

1 Heat the oil in a large saucepan and cook the onion and bacon until the onion is soft.

2 Add the carrot, zucchini, celery, potatoes, tomatoes and four-bean mix. Cook, stirring, for 1 minute.

3 Add 2.5 litres (87 fl oz/10 cups) of water to the pan. Bring to the boil, then reduce the heat and simmer, covered, for 1 hour.

4 Stir in the pasta and green beans. Simmer for 12 minutes, or until tender.

5 Sprinkle the minestrone with parmesan cheese and chopped parsley and serve with crusty bread.

Note: Prepare this recipe ahead of time and keep it in the refrigerator for warming winter after-school meals through the week or on weekends.

pea and ham soup

SERVES 4–6

2 tablespoons olive oil

2 onions, finely chopped

2 carrots, diced

2 celery sticks, diced

1 small turnip, finely chopped

440g (15½ oz) split green peas, rinsed and drained

1 smoked ham hock (800g/1 lb 12 oz)

2 bay leaves

2 sprigs thyme

½ teaspoon ground ginger

1 Heat the oil in a large saucepan over low heat. Add the onion, carrot, celery and turnip and cook for 5–6 minutes, or until softened.

2 Add the split peas, ham hock, bay leaves, thyme, ground ginger and 2.5 litres (87 fl oz/10 cups) of water. Bring to the boil over medium heat.

3 Reduce the heat and simmer, covered, for 2 hours 30 minutes to 3 hours.

4 Remove the ham bones and meat, then cut the meat into smaller pieces. Return to the soup.

5 Remove the bay leaves and thyme.

ham and pineapple pinwheels

MAKES ABOUT 24

2 sheets ready-rolled puff pastry

1 egg, lightly beaten

100 g (3½ oz) ham, thinly sliced

150 g (5½ oz) tinned crushed pineapple,
   well drained

40 g (1½ oz/⅓ cup) grated cheddar cheese

1 Preheat oven to 180°C (350°F/Gas 4).
   Lightly grease two large baking trays.

2 Lay out the pastry sheets. Brush with
   the beaten egg.

3 Sprinkle with the ham, pineapple
   and cheese.

4 Roll each sheet up firmly and evenly.
   Using a sharp serrated knife, cut each
   roll into 12 rounds.

5 Place the wheels on the baking trays.
   Bake for 15 minutes, or until golden
   and puffed. Serve warm or hot.

Note: This recipe can be made up
to 3 weeks in advance and stored
in freezer.

crunchy cheese bites

250 g (9 oz/2 cups) grated cheddar cheese

125 g (4^1/$_2$ oz) feta cheese, crumbled

60 g (2^1/$_4$ oz/^{1}/$_4$ cup) ricotta cheese

30 g (1 oz/^{1}/$_4$ cup) chopped spring onions (scallions)

1 small tomato, chopped

1 egg, beaten

5 sheets ready-rolled puff pastry

beaten egg, to brush

milk, to brush

1   Preheat the oven to 220°C (425°F/ Gas 7). Combine the cheeses, spring onion, tomato and egg in a bowl.

2   Cut the pastry into circles using a 10 cm (4 inch) cutter. Place heaped teaspoons of the mixture onto one half of each round.

3   Fold the pastry over the filling to make semi-circles. Brush the edges between the pastry with a little of the beaten egg and press the edges together firmly with a fork to seal.

4   Place on a baking tray and brush with a little milk. Bake in the oven for 10–15 minutes, or until puffed and golden. Allow the pastries to cool for at least 10 minutes before serving

cheese and ham subs

MAKES 4

2 hot dog rolls

215 g (7½ oz) tinned spaghetti in tomato and cheese sauce

50 g (1¾ oz) sliced ham, chopped

50 g (1¾ oz) cheddar cheese slices, cut into strips

1 Preheat oven to 180°C (350°F/Gas 4). Lightly grease a baking tray.

2 Cut the rolls in half horizontally and place on the tray.

3 Top each roll half with spaghetti, ham and cheese. Bake 12 minutes, or until the cheese melts and the bread is crispy.

chicken, corn and avocado melt

SERVES 2–4

4 thick slices bread

130 g (4¾ oz) tinned creamed corn

8 slices smoked chicken breast

1 avocado, sliced

2 teaspoons chopped chives

90 g (3¼ oz/¾ cup) grated cheddar cheese

1 Preheat the grill (broiler) to hot. Toast the bread lightly on both sides.

2 Spread the creamed corn onto each slice. Top with the chicken and avocado. Sprinkle with the chives and cheese.

3 Place under the grill and cook for 2 minutes, or until cheese is melted and bubbling. Serve immediately.

sticky chicken drumsticks

SERVES 4

2 tablespoons honey

2 tablespoons sweet chilli sauce

2 tablespoons tomato sauce (ketchup)

2 tablespoons dark soy sauce

2 tablespoons light soy sauce

1.5 kg (3 lb 5 oz) skinless chicken drumsticks

2 tablespoons sesame seeds

1. Put the honey, chilli sauce, tomato sauce and soy sauces in a large non-metallic dish and stir together. Cut 2–3 slits across each drumstick with a knife.

2. Coat the drumsticks in the marinade. Cover and refrigerate for at least 2 hours, or overnight. Turn in the marinade 2–3 times.

3. Preheat the oven to 180°C (350°F/Gas 4). Line a large baking tray with baking paper. Sprinkle the sesame seeds over the chicken and put them on the tray.

4. Bake for 45 minutes, or until cooked and golden, turning and brushing with the marinade 2–3 times. Serve warm or cold.

fresh spring rolls

MAKES 8

½ barbecued chicken

50 g (1¾ oz) dried mung bean vermicelli

8 x 17 cm (6½ inch) square dried rice paper wrappers

16 Thai basil leaves

1 large handful coriander (cilantro) leaves

1 carrot, cut into short thin strips and blanched

2 tablespoons plum sauce

1 Remove the meat from the chicken, discard the skin and finely shred the meat. Soak the vermicelli in hot water for 10 minutes and then drain.

2 Dip a rice paper wrapper into warm water for 10–15 seconds, or until it softens, then place it on a clean work surface. Put one-eighth of the chicken on the wrapper and top with two basil leaves, a few coriander leaves, a few carrot strips and a small amount of vermicelli. Spoon a little plum sauce over the top.

3 Press the filling down to flatten it a little, then fold in one side and roll it up tightly like a parcel. Lay the roll, seam side down, on a serving plate and sprinkle with a little water. Cover with a damp cloth and repeat with the remaining ingredients. Serve with your favourite dipping sauce or a little extra plum sauce.

mini quiche lorraines

MAKES 12

2 sheets frozen ready-rolled shortcrust (pie) pastry, thawed

1 tomato, chopped

60 g (2¼ oz/½ cup) grated cheddar cheese

40 g (1½ oz/¼ cup) chopped ham or bacon

1 spring onion (scallion), finely chopped

125 ml (4 fl oz/½ cup) milk

1 egg

1 Preheat the oven to 200°C (400°F/Gas 6).

2 Cut the pastry into 12 circles with an 8 cm (3¼ inch) cutter. Line 12 shallow patty pans or mini muffin tins with the pastry.

3 Mix together the tomato, cheese, ham and spring onion and spoon the mixture into the pastry cases.

4 Whisk together the milk and egg. Pour enough into each pastry case to cover the filling.

5 Bake for 15–20 minutes, or until the filling is set and golden. Transfer to a wire rack to cool. Store in the refrigerator in an airtight container for up to two days.

Variations: There are many different combinations of ingredients you can use. Try semi-dried (sun-blushed) tomatoes, feta and thyme; chopped black olives, ricotta and chicken; and tinned salmon, capers and cream cheese.

vegetable frittata squares with hummus

MAKES 30 PIECES

1 large red capsicum (pepper)

250 g (9 oz) orange sweet potato, cut into 1 cm (½ inch) slices

1½ tablespoons olive oil

1 leek, finely sliced

125 g (4½ oz) zucchini (courgettes), thinly sliced

300 g (10½ oz) eggplant (aubergines), cut into 1 cm (½ inch) slices

4 eggs, lightly beaten

1 tablespoon finely chopped basil

60 g (2¼ oz) grated parmesan cheese

100 g (3½ oz) ready-made hummus

1 Cut the capsicum into large pieces, removing the seeds and membrane. Place, skin side up, under a hot grill (broiler) until the skin blackens and blisters. Cool in a plastic bag. Peel.

2 Cook the sweet potato in a saucepan of boiling water for 4–5 minutes, or until just tender. Drain.

3 Heat 1 tablespoon of the oil in a frying pan. Add the leek and stir over medium heat for 1 minute, or until soft. Add the zucchini and cook for 2 minutes, then remove from the pan.

4 Heat the leftover oil. Cook the eggplant for 2 minutes each side, or until golden. Line the base of the pan with half the eggplant, then the leek and zucchini. Top with the capsicum, left-over eggplant and sweet potato.

5 Combine the eggs, basil, and parmesan. Pour the mixture over the vegetables. Cook over low heat for 15 minutes. Put the pan under a hot grill (broiler) until golden. Cool, then flip onto a chopping board. Cut into 30 squares. Top with hummus.

bean enchiladas

MAKES 4

2 teaspoons light olive oil

½ onion, thinly sliced

1 garlic clove, crushed

1 teaspoon ground cumin

3 tablespoons salt-reduced vegetable stock

2 tomatoes, peeled, deseeded and chopped

2 teaspoons tomato paste (concentrated purée)

425 g (15 oz) tinned three-bean mix, drained and rinsed

1 tablespoon chopped coriander (cilantro) leaves

4 flour tortillas

½ small avocado, chopped

60 g (2¼ oz) light sour cream

1 small handful coriander (cilantro) sprigs

60 g (2¼ oz) shredded lettuce

1 Preheat the oven to 170°C (325°F/Gas 3).

2 Heat the oil in a frying pan over medium heat. Add the onion and cook for 3–4 minutes, or until just soft. Add the garlic and cook for a further 30 seconds.

3 Add the cumin, vegetable stock, tomato and tomato paste and cook for 6–8 minutes, or until thick.

4 Add the beans to the sauce and cook for 5 minutes, then add the coriander.

5 Meanwhile, wrap the tortillas in foil and warm in the oven for 3–4 minutes.

6 Place a tortilla on a plate and spread with a large scoop of the bean mixture.

7 Top with some avocado, sour cream, coriander sprigs and lettuce. Roll the enchiladas up, tucking in the ends. Cut each one in half to serve.

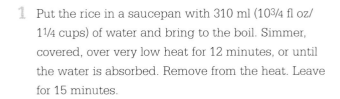

sushi hand rolls

MAKES 35

200 g (7 oz/1 cup) sushi rice

2 tablespoons white rice vinegar

1 tablespoon sugar

10 nori sheets, cut into quarters

sliced cucumber, pickled daikon, sliced avocado and blanched English spinach, to fill

1 Put the rice in a saucepan with 310 ml (10¾ fl oz/ 1¼ cups) of water and bring to the boil. Simmer, covered, over very low heat for 12 minutes, or until the water is absorbed. Remove from the heat. Leave for 15 minutes.

2 Mix the white rice vinegar, sugar and a pinch of salt, then stir through the rice. Leave to cool.

3 Cut the nori sheets into quarters.

4 Put 1½ tablespoons of rice in the middle of each nori square.

5 Top with 2–3 fillings from a selection of the fillings. Roll into a cone shape and serve with Japanese soy sauce for dipping.

Note: If you are making these rolls to eat at home, you can add fillings like sliced sashimi tuna, cooked prawns (shrimp), and fresh or smoked salmon. Don't pack these fillings in lunchboxes, for food safety reasons.

chicken pocket cones

MAKES 4

1 small pitta bread round

1 tablespoon cheese spread

1 tablespoon low-fat mayonnaise

4 slices chicken loaf, halved

chives, for tying cones

1 small Lebanese (short) cucumber, cut into small sticks

4 lettuce leaves, shredded

1 small tomato, finely chopped

1 Cut the pitta bread in half. Split the halves to make two semi-circles. Spread evenly with the cheese spread and the mayonnaise. Top each with a piece of chicken loaf.

2 Roll each semi-circle into a cone. Tie with a chive to hold the shape.

3 Stuff cones with a few cucumber sticks, some lettuce and top with the tomato. Refrigerate for at least 1 hour before serving.

falafel rollups

MAKES 4

4 spring onions (scallions), chopped

15 g (½ oz) roughly chopped flat-leaf (Italian) parsley

1 handful coriander (cilantro) leaves

1 teaspoon ground coriander

1 teaspoon ground cumin

pinch of chilli powder

1 garlic clove, crushed

150 g (5½ oz) tinned chickpeas, rinsed and drained

plain (all-purpose) flour, to coat

oil, for cooking

2 tablespoons ready-made hummus

2 rounds Lebanese bread, cut in half

100 g (3½ oz) ready-made tabouleh

1   Put the spring onion, parsley and coriander in a food processor, and process until finely chopped.

2   Add the spices, garlic and chickpeas, and process to a smooth paste.

3   Shape into 12 patties. Coat lightly in flour and refrigerate for 45 minutes.

4   Fill a deep heavy-based saucepan one-third full of oil and heat to 180°C (350°F), or until a bread cube browns in 15 seconds.

5   Cook the falafel in batches for 2–3 minutes, or until browned and cooked through. Drain on paper towels.

6   To serve, split the Lebanese bread halves. Spread the hummus over the bread, top with the tabouleh and three falafel each. Roll up and wrap in baking paper.

ratatouille tarts

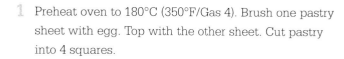

MAKES 4 TARTS

2 sheets ready-rolled puff pastry

1 egg, lightly beaten

1 tablespoon olive oil

1 onion, finely sliced

2 garlic cloves, crushed

2 long slender eggplant (aubergine), cut into thin slices

2 zucchini (courgettes), cut into thin slices

1 red capsicum (pepper), diced

2 tomatoes, roughly chopped

1 Preheat oven to 180°C (350°F/Gas 4). Brush one pastry sheet with egg. Top with the other sheet. Cut pastry into 4 squares.

2 Place on a large baking tray and cook for 20 minutes, until puffed and golden. Set aside to cool.

3 Heat the oil in a large heavy-based frying pan. Cook the onion and garlic over medium heat for 5 minutes. Add the eggplant, zucchini and capsicum. Cook, covered, for 10 minutes, stirring occasionally.

4 Add the tomatoes and cook, uncovered, for about 10 minutes, stirring.

5 Cut an 8 cm (3¼ inch) round hole in each of the pastry squares, and pull out the soft pastry in the centre.

6 Fill each of the holes with vegetable mixture.

quesadillas

MAKES 4

1 tablespoon oil

500 g (1 lb 2 oz) minced (ground) chicken

35 g (1¼ oz) packet taco seasoning mix

125 g (4½ oz/½ cup) tomato salsa

230 g (8½ oz/1 cup) tinned refried beans

250 g (9 oz/2 cups) grated low-fat tasty cheese

4 flour tortillas

sour cream, to serve

1. Heat the oil in a frying pan and cook the chicken, using a fork to break up any lumps.

2. Add the taco seasoning and stir, cooking for 2 minutes. Add the salsa. Stir until warmed through. Remove from the heat.

3. In a small saucepan, heat the refried beans with 4 tablespoons of water until the mixture is thick.

4. To make the quesadillas, put some of the cheese on half of each tortilla. Top with the chicken mixture, refried beans and more cheese.

5. Fold the top over and cook each one in a frying pan over medium heat until browned on both sides. Serve with a dollop of sour cream.

vegetable filo pouches

SERVES 4

oil spray

8 sheets filo pastry

80 g (2¾ oz/½ cup) sesame seeds

filling

450 g (1 lb/3 cups) grated carrot

2 large onions, finely chopped

1 tablespoon grated fresh ginger

1 tablespoon finely chopped coriander (cilantro) leaves

225 g (8 oz/1⅓ cups) tinned water chestnuts, rinsed and sliced

1 tablespoon white miso paste

3 tablespoons tahini paste

1 Preheat the oven to 180°C (350°F/ Gas 4). Spray two baking trays with oil.

2 To make the filling, combine the carrot, onion, ginger, coriander and 250 ml (9 fl oz/1 cup) of water in a large pan. Cover and cook over low heat for 20 minutes.

3 Uncover, cook for a further 5 minutes, or until all the liquid has evaporated. Remove from the heat and cool slightly. Stir in the water chestnuts, miso and tahini.

4 Spray one sheet of filo pastry with oil. Top with another three pastry sheets, spraying between each layer.

5 Cut the pastry into six squares. Repeat the process with the remaining pastry sheets.

6 Divide the filling evenly between each square, placing the filling in the centre. Bring the edges together and pinch to form a pouch.

7 Spray each pouch with oil, then press in the sesame seeds. Place on the trays and bake for 10–12 minutes, or until golden brown.

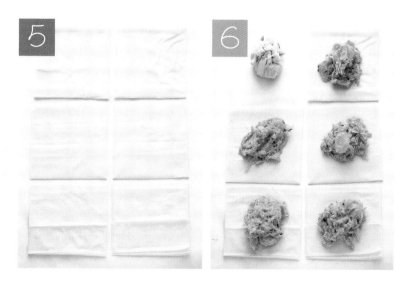

vegetable and noodle stir-fry

SERVES 2

60 g (2¼ oz) cellophane or egg noodles

1 teaspoon oil

½ carrot, cut into sticks

½ celery stalk, chopped

½ small zucchini (courgette), halved lengthways, sliced

½ red capsicum (pepper), deseeded, cut into sticks

40 g (1½ oz) cauliflower florets

40 g (1½ oz) broccoli florets

30 g (1 oz) green beans, sliced

½ garlic clove, crushed

1 tablespoon salt-reduced soy sauce

1   Put the noodles in a bowl. Cover with boiling water. Leave to stand for 1 minute, or until tender. Drain.

2   Heat the oil in a wok or frying pan. Add the carrot, celery, zucchini, capsicum, cauliflower, broccoli, beans and garlic and stir-fry for 4–5 minutes.

3   Toss the noodles through the vegetables with the soy sauce. Stir-fry for another minute.

chicken noodle omelette

SERVES 2

85 g (3 oz) packet chicken-flavoured instant noodles

175 g (6 oz/1 cup) chopped cooked chicken

2 teaspoons finely chopped flat-leaf (Italian) parsley

2 eggs, lightly beaten

2 tablespoons grated cheddar cheese

1   Boil 500 ml (17 fl oz/2 cups) of water in a saucepan. Add the noodles and flavour sachet to the saucepan. Cook the noodles as directed. Drain well.

2   Put the noodles, chicken, parsley and eggs in a bowl. Mix well.

3   Put the mixture in a 20 cm (8 inch) non-stick frying pan. Cook for 5 minutes without stirring.

4   Sprinkle with the cheese. Put under a hot grill (broiler) and grill (broil) for 2 minutes, or until browned. Serve hot.

tuna enchiladas

MAKES 8

1 tablespoon light olive oil

1 onion, thinly sliced

3 garlic cloves, crushed

2 teaspoons ground cumin

125 ml (4 fl oz/1/2 cup) vegetable stock

425 g (15 oz) tinned tuna in brine, drained

3 tomatoes, peeled, deseeded and chopped

1 tablespoon tomato paste (concentrated purée)

425 g (15 oz) tinned three-bean mix

2 tablespoons chopped coriander (cilantro) leaves

8 flour tortillas

1 small avocado, chopped

125 g (4 1/2 oz/1/2 cup) light sour cream

1 handful coriander (cilantro) sprigs

115 g (4 oz/2 cups) shredded lettuce

1 Preheat the oven to 170°C (325°F/Gas 3). Heat the oil in a deep frying pan over medium heat. Add the onion and cook for 3–4 minutes, or until just soft. Add the garlic and cook for another 30 seconds. Add the cumin, vegetable stock, tuna, tomato and tomato paste and cook for 6–8 minutes, or until the mixture is thick.

2 Drain and rinse the bean mix. Add the beans to the sauce and cook for 5 minutes to heat through, then add the chopped coriander.

3 Meanwhile, wrap the tortillas in foil and warm in the oven for 3–4 minutes.

4 Place a tortilla on a plate and spread with a large scoop of the bean mixture. Top with some avocado, sour cream, coriander sprigs and lettuce. Roll the enchiladas up, tucking in the ends.

pitta pizzas

SERVES 4

4 large wholemeal (whole-wheat) pitta pocket breads

130 g (4³/₄ oz/¹/₂ cup) tomato salsa

¹/₂ red onion, thinly sliced

90 g (3¹/₄ oz) mushrooms, thinly sliced

60 g (2¹/₄ oz) low-fat ham, thinly sliced

90 g (3¹/₄ oz/¹/₂ cup) black olives in brine, rinsed, drained, pitted and chopped

1 tablespoon capers, rinsed, drained and chopped

80 g (2³/₄ oz/¹/₂ cup) low-fat feta cheese

10 g (¹/₄ oz/¹/₄ cup) sprigs rosemary

100 g (3¹/₂ oz/1 cup) grated reduced-fat mozzarella

1 Preheat the oven to 200°C (400°F/Gas 6). Place the pitta breads on a baking tray.

2 Spread each with the salsa. Top with the onion, mushrooms, ham, olives and capers.

3 Crumble the feta over and top with the rosemary sprigs and mozzarella. Bake for 20 minutes.

Variations: Try the following toppings: low-fat ham, pineapple pieces, sliced capsicum (pepper), onion or olives marinated in brine.

For a meaty topping, try leftover savoury minced (ground) beef or spaghetti bolognaise and low-fat cheddar cheese.

For a little spice, try salami, corn kernels, sliced green capsicum, onion, tomato and low-fat feta cheese.

A tasty vegetarian option is artichoke hearts, tomato and zucchini (courgette) slices, ricotta and low-fat feta cheese.

party sausage rolls

MAKES 36

3 sheets frozen puff pastry, thawed

2 eggs, lightly beaten

750 g (1 lb 10 oz) minced (ground) sausage

1 onion, finely chopped

1 garlic clove, crushed

80 g (2¾ oz/1 cup) fresh breadcrumbs

3 tablespoons chopped flat-leaf (Italian) parsley

3 tablespoons chopped thyme

½ teaspoon ground sage

½ teaspoon freshly grated nutmeg

½ teaspoon ground cloves

½ teaspoon black pepper

1. Preheat the oven to 200°C (400°F/Gas 6). Lightly grease two baking trays.

2. Cut the pastry sheets in half and lightly brush the edges with some of the beaten egg.

3. To make the filling, mix half the remaining egg with the rest of the ingredients in a large bowl. Divide into six even portions.

4. Spoon the filling down the centre of each piece of pastry, then brush the edges with some of the egg.

5. Fold the pastry over the filling, overlapping the edges and placing the join underneath. Brush the rolls with more egg, then cut each into six short pieces. Cut two small slashes on top of each roll.

6. Place on the baking trays and bake for 15 minutes. Reduce the heat to 180°C (350°F/Gas 4) and bake for another 15 minutes, or until puffed and golden.

cheese pinwheels

MAKES ABOUT 12

125 g (4¹/₂ oz/1 cup) grated cheddar cheese

60 g (2¹/₄ oz) feta cheese, crumbled

1 tablespoon ricotta cheese

15 g (¹/₂ oz) chopped spring onions (scallions)

¹/₂ small tomato, chopped

1 egg, beaten

2 sheets ready-rolled puff pastry

milk, to brush

1 Preheat the oven to 220°C (425°F/Gas 7). Line a baking tray with baking paper.

2 Combine the cheeses, spring onion, tomato and two-thirds of the egg in a bowl.

3 Divide the cheese mixture into two and spread over 2 sheets of puff pastry, leaving a 1 cm (¹/₂ inch) border.

4 Roll up and trim the ends. Cut into 1.5 cm (5/8 inch) wheels and place on the baking tray. Brush with the leftover egg.

5 Bake for 12–15 minutes, or until puffed and golden. Cool for 5 minutes, then put on a wire rack to cool. Store in an airtight container.

sun-dried tomato plaits

MAKES 8

1 sheet frozen puff pastry, thawed

1 egg, beaten

40 g (1¹/₂ oz) semi-dried (sun-blushed) tomatoes, sliced

1 Preheat the oven to 210°C (415°F/Gas 6–7). Lightly grease a baking tray.

2 Lightly brush the puff pastry with the egg. Cut into 1 cm (¹/₂ inch) strips.

3 Join three strips together at the top, by pressing. Plait them together, putting slices of semi-dried tomato in the plait.

4 Place the plaits on the baking tray and bake for 10–15 minutes, or until puffed and golden. Cool for 5 minutes, then put on a wire rack to cool. Store in an airtight container.

beef and bean burritos

MAKES 8

2 tablespoons oil

1 onion, sliced

1 tablespoon ground cumin

2 teaspoons ground coriander

1/2 teaspoon ground cinnamon

1 teaspoon chilli powder

600 g (1 lb 5 oz) minced (ground) beef

425 g (15 oz) tomatoes, chopped

4 tablespoons tomato paste
(concentrated purée)

440 g (15 1/2 oz) tinned kidney beans, drained

270 g (9 1/2 oz) tinned corn kernels, drained

8 flour tortillas

Topping

160 g (5 3/4 oz) cheddar cheese, grated

3 tablespoons taco sauce (if you like)

1 Heat the oil in a large heavy-based frying pan. Add the onion, spices and beef. Cook over medium–high heat for 10 minutes until well browned and almost all the liquid has evaporated. Use a fork to break up any lumps of the minced beef as it cooks. Reduce the heat to low and add the tomatoes and paste. Cover and cook, stirring occasionally, for 20 minutes. Add the kidney beans and corn and stir until heated through.

2 Preheat the oven to 180°C (350°F/Gas 4). To assemble the burritos, place about 1/2 cup of minced beef mixture on each tortilla. Roll the tortillas around the filling and place, seam-side down, on a baking tray.

3 Sprinkle the burritos with the grated cheese. Bake for 10 minutes, or until the cheese has melted. Top each burrito with taco sauce, if you like, and serve immediately.

petit croque-monsieur

MAKES 24

16 slices white bread

125 g (4½ oz/½ cup) wholegrain mustard

100 g (3½ oz) thinly shaved honey ham

100 g (3½ oz) Jarlsberg cheese, thinly sliced

40 g (1½ oz) butter

2 tablespoons olive oil

1 Spread each slice of bread with mustard. Lay out eight bread slices on a board, mustard-side-up. Top with the shaved ham, then the cheese slices.

2 Press the remaining bread slices on top, mustard side down, to make eight sandwiches. Trim off the crusts, then cut each sandwich into three fingers.

3 Melt half the butter and oil in a non-stick frying pan. When the butter begins to foam, cook half the fingers until crisp and golden on both sides and the cheese is just starting to melt. Remove and keep warm on a baking tray in the oven. Melt the remaining butter and oil in the frying pan and cook the remaining fingers. Serve warm.

vegetarian chilli

130 g (4¹/₂ oz/³/₄ cup) burghul (bulgur)

2 tablespoons olive oil

1 onion, finely chopped

2 garlic cloves, crushed

2 teaspoons ground cumin

1 teaspoon chilli powder

¹/₂ teaspoon ground cinnamon

820 g (1 lb 13 oz) tinned crushed tomatoes

750 ml (26 fl oz/3 cups) vegetable stock

440 g (15¹/₂ oz) tinned red kidney beans, rinsed and drained

440 g (15¹/₂ oz) tinned chickpeas, rinsed and drained

315 g (11 oz) tinned corn kernels, rinsed and drained

2 tablespoons tomato paste (concentrated purée)

plain yoghurt, to serve

1 Put the burghul in a heatproof bowl and pour in 250 ml (9 fl oz/1 cup) of hot water. Leave to stand until needed.

2 Heat the oil in a large saucepan and add the onion. Cook for about 10 minutes over medium heat, stirring occasionally, or until soft and lightly golden. Add the garlic, cumin, chilli and cinnamon and stir-fry for 1 minute.

3 Add the burghul and all the remaining ingredients, except the yoghurt, and stir to combine. Reduce the heat to low and simmer for 30 minutes. Serve with a dollop of yoghurt.

leek and cheese frittata

SERVES 6

2 tablespoons olive oil

3 leeks, white part only, thinly sliced

2 zucchini (courgettes), thinly sliced

1 garlic clove, crushed

5 eggs, lightly beaten

4 tablespoons grated parmesan cheese

4 tablespoons diced Swiss cheese

1 Heat 1 tablespoon of the olive oil in a small frying pan. Add the leek and cook, stirring, over low heat until slightly softened. Cover and cook the leek for 10 minutes, stirring occasionally. Add the zucchini and garlic and cook for another 10 minutes. Transfer the mixture to a bowl. Allow to cool, then season with pepper. Add the egg and cheeses and stir through.

2 Heat the remaining oil in the pan, then add the egg mixture and smooth the surface. Cook over low heat for 15 minutes, or until the frittata is almost set.

3 Put the pan under a hot grill (broiler) for 3–5 minutes, or until the top is set and golden. Allow the frittata to stand for 5 minutes before cutting into wedges and serving. Serve with a fresh green salad.

corn and capsicum fritters

SERVES 4

4 tablespoons oil

300 g (10½ oz/1½ cups) tinned corn kernels, drained

1 large red capsicum (pepper), chopped

2 tablespoons chopped flat-leaf (Italian) parsley

3 eggs, beaten

sour cream, to serve

1 Heat 2 tablespoons of oil in a frying pan over medium heat. Add the corn and cook, stirring, for 2 minutes. Add the capsicum and stir for another 2 minutes. Put in a bowl. Add the parsley and mix.

2 Stir the beaten egg into the vegetable mixture.

3 Heat another 2 tablespoons of oil in a non-stick frying pan over medium heat. Drop large tablespoons of the mixture into the pan. Cook for 1–2 minutes, or until golden brown. Turn and cook the other side.

4 Drain on paper towels. Serve with sour cream and a green salad.

potato and leek fritters

MAKES 40

600 g (1 lb 5 oz) all-purpose potatoes, peeled and grated

1 leek, finely chopped

2 eggs, lightly beaten

1 tablespoon rice flour

2 tablespoons canola oil

1 Put the potato and leek in a bowl. Add the eggs and rice flour and mix.

2 Heat the oil in a large non-stick frying pan. Drop tablespoons of the mixture into the pan. Cook for 1–2 minutes, or until golden brown. Turn and cook the other side.

3 Drain on paper towels. Serve cold either on their own or with baked beans.

pasta with chicken and asparagus

SERVES 2

2 tablespoons canola oil

2 small skinless chicken breast fillets, sliced

1/2 small leek, halved lengthways, thinly sliced

1 garlic clove, crushed

75 g (21/2 oz) green beans, diagonally sliced into 3 cm (11/4 inch) pieces

75 g (21/2 oz) asparagus, trimmed and sliced into 3 cm (11/4 inch) pieces

125 ml (4 fl oz/1/2 cup) chicken stock

150 g (51/2 oz) pasta (we used large spiral pasta)

1 Heat 1 tablespoon of the oil in a large non-stick frying pan over medium heat. Cook the chicken for 4 minutes on each side, or until cooked through.

2 Heat the remaining oil in the pan. Add the leek and cook, stirring often, for 6–7 minutes or until almost soft. Add the garlic, beans and asparagus.

3 Cook for 2–3 minutes, or until the vegetables are tender. Increase the heat to high and pour in the stock. Simmer for 2–3 minutes, or until the liquid reduces slightly.

4 Meanwhile, cook the pasta in a large saucepan of boiling water for 12 minutes, or until just tender. Drain and return to the pan.

5 Add the chicken to the pasta along with the vegetables and sauce and toss.

vegetable couscous

SERVES 4

15 g (1/2 oz) unsalted butter

1/2 onion, sliced

1/2 garlic clove, crushed

1/2 teaspoon ground cumin

1 carrot, thinly sliced

75 g (2 1/2 oz) pumpkin (winter squash), chopped

150 g (5 1/2 oz) tinned chickpeas, drained

200 g (7 oz) tinned chopped tomatoes

1/2 all-purpose potato, chopped

1 small eggplant (aubergine), chopped

1 1/2 tablespoons vegetable stock

75 g (2 1/2 oz) green beans, cut into short lengths

1 zucchini (courgette), cut into chunks

couscous

125 ml (4 fl oz/1/2 cup) salt-reduced vegetable stock

90 g (3 1/4 oz) instant couscous

15 g (1/2 oz) unsalted butter

1 Melt the butter in a saucepan over medium heat. Add the onion, garlic and cumin and cook for 2–3 minutes, or until softened.

2 Add the carrot, pumpkin, chickpeas, tomato, potato, eggplant and vegetable stock. Cook for 10 minutes, stirring occasionally.

3 Add the beans and zucchini and cook for another 5 minutes, or until the vegetables are tender.

4 To make the couscous, pour the stock into a saucepan and add 3 tablespoons of water. Bring to the boil. Remove from the heat and stir in the couscous and butter. Cover and stand for 5 minutes. Fluff the grains with a fork.

5 Fold the vegetables through the couscous.

mini shepherd's pies

MAKES 4

1 tablespoon oil

500 g (1 lb 2 oz) minced (ground) steak

2 tablespoons plain (all-purpose) flour

250 ml (9 fl oz/1 cup) salt-reduced beef stock

2 tablespoons chopped flat-leaf (Italian) parsley

4 all-purpose potatoes, cooked

3 tablespoons milk

15 g (1/2 oz) unsalted butter

135 g (4 3/4 oz/1 cup) frozen mixed vegetables (peas, beans, carrots), thawed

60 g (2 1/4 oz/1/2 cup) grated cheese

3 tablespoons dried breadcrumbs

1 Preheat the oven to 180°C (350°F/Gas 4). Heat the oil in a frying pan over medium heat. Add the meat and brown, breaking the meat up with a spoon.

2 Stir in the flour and cook, stirring, for 1 minute.

3 Blend in the stock and parsley. Simmer, stirring, for about 5 minutes, or until the mixture thickens.

4 Mash the potatoes well. Add the milk and butter and beat until smooth, adding more of each if needed.

5 Spoon the meat mixture into four 200 ml (7 fl oz) ovenproof bowls.

6 Top with the mixed vegetables and spread the mashed potato over the top.

7 Mix together the cheese and breadcrumbs and sprinkle over each pie. Bake in the oven for 10–15 minutes, or until the tops are golden.

oven chips

SERVES 6

6 all-purpose potatoes

3 tablespoons olive oil

1. Preheat the oven to 220°C (425°F/Gas 7). Cut the potatoes into slices about 1 cm (1/2 inch) thick.

2. Soak the chips (fries) in cold water for 10 minutes. Drain well, then pat dry with paper towels.

3. Spread the chips onto a baking tray and sprinkle the oil over them. Toss to coat.

4. Bake for 45–55 minutes until golden and crisp, turning occasionally.

oven-baked chicken nuggets

SERVES 4

90 g (3¼ oz) cornflakes

400 g (14 oz) chicken breast fillets, cut into bite-sized pieces

2 egg whites, lightly beaten

canola spray

1. Preheat the oven to 200°C (400°F/Gas 6). Lightly spray a baking tray with canola spray.

2. Put the cornflakes in a food processor and process until the mixture forms fine crumbs. Put in a bowl.

3. Toss the chicken pieces in the seasoned flour, then in the egg white. Roll each piece in the crumbs until well coated.

4. Put the nuggets on the baking tray. Bake for 10–12 minutes, or until lightly browned.

strawberry shake

175 g (6 oz/1 cup) chopped strawberries
(or raspberries)

250 ml (9 fl oz/1 cup) milk

3 scoops vanilla or strawberry ice cream

sugar, to taste, if using raspberries

1 Put the strawberries or raspberries, milk
   and ice cream (and sugar, if using) into
   a blender and blend until smooth.

2 Pour into two cups and serve.

banana smoothie

SERVES 2

1 banana, roughly chopped

1 tablespoon plain yoghurt

1 teaspoon honey

250 ml (9 fl oz/1 cup) milk

1 Put the banana in a blender with the
   yoghurt, honey and milk and blend until
   smooth, thick and creamy.

2 Pour into two cups and serve.

berry froth

SERVES 2

220 g (7³/₄ oz/1²/₃ cup) fresh or frozen mixed berries

500 ml (17 fl oz/2 cups) milk

2 ice cubes

sugar, to taste

1 Put the mixed berries, milk and ice cubes in
   a blender and blend until smooth. Add the
   sugar and blend again until combined.

2 Pour into two large cups and serve.

fresh fruit slushy

SERVES 4

90 g (3¹/₄ oz) fresh pineapple, peeled and cored,
cut into chunks

1 banana, cut into chunks

3 kiwi fruit, sliced

250 ml (9 fl oz/1 cup) tropical fruit juice

2 ice cubes

1 Put the pineapple and banana in a blender
   with the kiwi fruit, fruit juice and ice cubes
   and blend until smooth.

2 Pour into four cups and serve.

dinnertime

jacket potatoes

MAKES 4

4 large potatoes

avocado, tomato and corn salsa filling

2 tomatoes, chopped

125 g (4½ oz) tinned corn kernels

2 spring onions (scallions), chopped

1 tablespoon lime juice

½ teaspoon sugar

1 avocado, diced

1 small handful coriander (cilantro) leaves, chopped

1 tablespoon low-fat sour cream

mushroom and bacon filling

3 bacon slices, finely sliced

2 spring onions (scallions), chopped

1 garlic clove, crushed

1 teaspoon chopped thyme

180 g (6 oz/2 cups) sliced button mushrooms

185 g (6½ oz/¾ cup) low-fat sour cream

2 tablespoons chopped flat-leaf (Italian) parsley

grated low-fat cheese, to serve

1 Preheat the oven to 210°C (415°F/Gas 6–7). Pierce potatoes all over with a fork. Put the potatoes on an oven rack. Bake for 1 hour, or until tender.

2 Cut a cross in the top of each potato and squeeze gently to open (you may need to hold the hot potatoes in a clean tea towel as you do this).

3 To make the avocado salsa filling, put the tomatoes, corn kernels, spring onions, lime juice and sugar in a bowl. Mix well, then add the avocado and coriander leaves. Spoon over the baked potatoes, along with some sour cream, if desired.

4 To make the mushroom filling, cook the bacon in a frying pan over medium heat until lightly golden. Add the spring onions, garlic clove, thyme and button mushrooms. Cook for 3–4 minutes over high heat. Add the sour cream. Reduce the heat to low and cook for another minute. Add the parsley, then spoon the mixture over the baked potatoes. Sprinkle with grated cheese.

stuffed capsicums

SERVES 4

4 small red capsicums (peppers)

110 g (3³/₄ oz/¹/₂ cup) short-grain white rice

1 tablespoon olive oil

1 onion, finely chopped

2 garlic cloves, crushed

1 tomato, chopped

125 g (4¹/₂ oz/1 cup) finely grated cheddar cheese

25 g (1 oz/¹/₄ cup) finely grated parmesan cheese

1 handful basil, chopped

1 handful flat-leaf (Italian) parsley, chopped

1. Preheat the oven to 180°C (350°F/Gas 4). Cut the tops off the capsicums and scoop out the seeds and white membranes.

2. Cook the rice in a large saucepan of boiling water until tender. Drain well and set aside to cool.

3. Heat the oil in a frying pan and cook the onion for a few minutes until lightly golden. Add the garlic and cook for 1 more minute.

4. Add the onion and garlic to the rice, along with all the remaining ingredients. Mix everything together well and season with salt and pepper.

5. Spoon the rice filling into the capsicums and place on a baking tray. Bake for 30 minutes, or until the capsicums are soft and the filling is brown on top.

stuffed mushrooms

SERVES 4-6

8 large flat or 12 button mushrooms

2 tablespoons oil

1 small onion, finely chopped

4 bacon slices, chopped

80 g (2³/₄ oz/1 cup) fresh breadcrumbs

1 tablespoon chopped flat-leaf (Italian) parsley

65 g (2¹/₄ oz/²/₃ cup) grated parmesan cheese

1. Preheat the oven to 180°C (350°F/Gas 4). Brush a baking tray with melted butter or oil.

2. Remove the stems of the mushrooms. Finely chop the stems.

3. Heat the oil in a frying pan, add the onion and bacon and cook until the bacon is lightly browned. Add the chopped mushroom stems and cook for 1 minute.

4. Transfer the mixture to a bowl. Add the breadcrumbs, parsley and parmesan and stir to combine.

5. Place the mushroom caps onto the baking tray and spoon the filling into the caps. Bake for 20 minutes, or until the mushrooms are tender and the topping is golden. Serve immediately.

potato salad

600 g (1 lb 5 oz) all-purpose potatoes

½ small red onion, finely chopped

2–3 celery stalks, finely chopped

1 small green capsicum (pepper), chopped

2 tablespoons finely chopped flat-leaf (Italian) parsley

dressing

185 g (6½ oz/¾ cup) mayonnaise

1–2 tablespoons white vinegar or lemon juice

2 tablespoons sour cream

1 Wash and peel the potatoes. Cut into small pieces. Cook the potato in a large saucepan of boiling water for about 5 minutes, or until just tender. Drain the potato and allow it to cool.

2 Combine the onion, celery, capsicum and parsley in a large bowl. Add the cooled potato.

3 To make the dressing, mix together the mayonnaise, vinegar or juice and sour cream. Season with salt and pepper.

4 Pour the dressing over the potato and gently toss to combine.

scalloped potatoes

SERVES 4

500 g (1 lb 2 oz) all-purpose potatoes

170 ml (5½ fl oz/⅔ cup) milk

125 ml (4 fl oz/½ cup) cream

60 g (2¼ oz/½ cup) grated cheddar cheese

20 g (¾ oz) butter

1 Preheat the oven to 180°C (350°F/Gas 4). Brush a 20 cm (8 inch) shallow ovenproof dish with melted butter or oil.

2 Peel the potatoes and cut into thin slices. Layer the slices in the dish, overlapping them slightly.

3 Combine the milk and the cream and drizzle over the potato.

4 Sprinkle the cheese evenly over the potato, then dot with the butter. Bake for 45 minutes, or until the potato is tender and the top is golden brown.

pizza

SERVES 4

1 large fresh or frozen pizza base

tomato sauce

1 tablespoon olive oil

1 small onion, chopped

1 garlic clove, crushed

1 large tomato, chopped

1 tablespoon tomato paste (concentrated purée)

1/2 teaspoon dried oregano

napolitana topping

grated mozzarella cheese, chopped dried oregano, sliced pitted black olives and thinly sliced anchovy fillets (optional)

pepperoni topping

red capsicum (pepper), pepperoni and grated mozzarella cheese

1 To make the tomato sauce, heat the olive oil in a small saucepan over medium heat and add the onion and garlic. Cook for 3 minutes, or until soft.

2 Add the chopped tomato and stir to combine. Reduce the heat to low and simmer for 10 minutes, stirring occasionally.

3 Stir in the tomato paste and oregano and simmer for another 2 minutes. Set aside to cool.

4 Preheat the oven to 220°C (425°F/Gas 7). Put the pizza base on a non-stick pizza tray or a large baking tray lined with baking paper. Spread the tomato sauce over the pizza base.

5 Top with your favourite topping to make either a napolitana or pepperoni pizza. Bake for 30 minutes.

quick pasta with tomato sauce

SERVES 4

1 tablespoon extra virgin olive oil

1 garlic clove, crushed

400 g (14 oz) tinned chopped tomatoes

500 g (1 lb 2 oz) penne

1 tablespoon grated parmesan cheese

1 Heat the olive oil in a frying pan over medium heat. Cook the garlic, stirring constantly, for 30 seconds. Add the tomatoes and stir through. Reduce the heat to low and cook for a further 8–10 minutes, stirring occasionally, or until reduced.

2 Meanwhile, cook the pasta in a large saucepan of boiling water until just tender. Drain and return to the saucepan.

3 Add the cooked tomatoes to the pasta and stir through. Spoon into bowls and sprinkle with parmesan cheese.

fettucine carbonara

SERVES 4

2 teaspoons oil

8 bacon slices, cut into thin strips

500 g (1 lb 2 oz) fettucine

4 eggs

50 g (1³/₄ oz/¹/₂ cup) grated parmesan cheese

250 ml (9 fl oz/1 cup) cream

1 Heat the oil in a frying pan and cook the bacon over medium heat until brown and crisp. Remove from the pan and drain on paper towels.

2 Add the fettucine to a large saucepan of boiling water and cook until just tender. Drain well in a colander, then return to the pan.

3 Put the eggs, cheese and cream into a small bowl and beat together with a fork. Add the bacon.

4 Pour the sauce over the hot pasta. Stir over very low heat for 1 minute, or until the sauce thickens.

lasagne

SERVES 6

1 tablespoon olive oil

1 large onion, finely chopped

3 large garlic cloves, crushed

1 celery stalk, diced

1 carrot, diced

125 g (4½ oz) button mushrooms, sliced

500 g (1 lb 2 oz) lean minced (ground) beef

1 teaspoon dried oregano

250 ml (9 fl oz/1 cup) red wine or water

500 ml (17 fl oz/2 cups) beef stock

2 tablespoons tomato paste (concentrated purée)

800 g (1 lb 12 oz) tinned chopped tomatoes

500 g (1 lb 2 oz) English spinach

20 g (¾ oz) butter

4 tablespoons plain (all-purpose) flour

375 ml (13 fl oz/1½ cups) milk

150 g (5½ oz/⅔ cup) ricotta cheese

375 g (13 oz) fresh lasagne sheets

85 g (3 oz/⅔ cup) grated cheddar cheese

1. Heat the oil in a large pan over high heat. Add the onion and cook for 2 minutes. Add the garlic, celery, carrot and mushrooms and cook for 2 minutes. Add the beef and cook for 5 minutes, or until cooked. Add the oregano and cook for 3–4 minutes.

2. Add the wine, stock, tomato paste and tomatoes and season. Reduce the heat to low and simmer, covered, for 1½ hours, stirring occasionally. Cool slightly. Wilt the washed spinach for 1 minute in a covered pan.

3. To make the white sauce, melt the butter in a saucepan over medium heat. Stir in the flour and cook for 1 minute. Slowly stir in the milk, and keep stirring until the sauce boils and thickens. Simmer for 2 minutes. Stir in the ricotta until smooth.

4. Preheat the oven to 200°C (400°F/Gas 6). Arrange a third of the pasta over the base of a large ovenproof dish. Spread with half the beef, then half the spinach. Make another layer of pasta and spread with the remaining beef, then the spinach, then the remaining pasta. Top with the white sauce, sprinkle with cheddar and bake for 30 minutes, or until golden.

spaghetti with chicken meatballs

SERVES 4

tomato sauce

1 teaspoon olive oil

2 garlic cloves, crushed

800 g (1 lb 12 oz) tinned crushed tomatoes

chicken meatballs

500 g (1 lb 2 oz) minced (ground) chicken

2 garlic cloves, crushed

20 g (³/₄ oz/¹/₄ cup) fresh breadcrumbs

2 tablespoons chopped basil

¹/₄ teaspoon cayenne pepper

1 tablespoon olive oil

2 tablespoons chopped basil

375 g (13 oz) spaghetti

30 g (1 oz) parmesan cheese, grated

1. To make the tomato sauce, heat the oil in a large non-stick saucepan over medium heat. Add the garlic and cook for 1 minute, or until just turning golden. Add the tomatoes and season. Reduce the heat and simmer for 15 minutes, or until thickened.

2. Line a baking tray with baking paper. To make the meatballs, combine the chicken, garlic, breadcrumbs, basil and cayenne pepper in a large bowl and season.

3. Using damp hands, roll tablespoons of the mixture into balls and place on the tray.

4. Heat the olive oil in a frying pan over medium heat. Cook the meatballs in batches, turning, for 3–4 minutes, or until golden. Transfer the meatballs to the sauce and simmer for a further 10 minutes, or until cooked through. Add the basil.

5. Meanwhile, cook the spaghetti in a large saucepan of boiling water for 10 minutes, or until tender. Drain well. Toss the spaghetti with the meatballs and sauce and serve with the grated parmesan.

spinach and ricotta cannelloni

SERVES 4

20 g (³/₄ oz) unsalted butter

1 small onion, finely chopped

2 garlic cloves, crushed

3 bunches English spinach

300 g (10¹/₂ oz/1¹/₄ cups) ricotta cheese

1 tablespoon dried oregano

tomato sauce

1 tablespoon olive oil

1 small onion, finely chopped

2 garlic cloves, crushed

440 g (15¹/₂ oz) tinned tomatoes

125 ml (4 fl oz/¹/₂ cup) tomato pasta sauce

1 teaspoon dried oregano

2 teaspoons dijon mustard

1 tablespoon balsamic vinegar

1 teaspoon sugar

375 g (13 oz) fresh lasagne sheets

70 g (2¹/₂ oz) grated mozzarella cheese

50 g (1³/₄ oz) grated parmesan cheese

1. Preheat the oven to 180°C (350°F/Gas 4). To make the filling, melt the butter in a saucepan and cook the onion and garlic for 3–5 minutes until softened. Shred the spinach, add to the pan and cook for 5 minutes, or until wilted and the moisture has evaporated. Remove from the heat and leave to cool. Put in a blender with the ricotta and oregano and process until smooth.

2. To make the sauce, heat the oil in a saucepan and cook the onion and garlic over low heat for 5 minutes. Add the rest of the sauce ingredients. Bring to the boil, then simmer for 10 minutes, or until thick.

3. Cut the lasagne sheets into twelve 12 cm (4¹/₂ inch) squares. Lightly grease a large ovenproof dish and spread a third of the sauce over the base.

4. Spoon spinach filling down the side of each lasagne square, then roll up the pasta around the filling and put, seam side down, in the dish. Space out the cannelloni evenly, then spread the remaining sauce over the top. Sprinkle with grated mozzarella and parmesan and bake for 30–35 minutes, or until golden.

potato gnocchi with tomato sauce

SERVES 4–6

tomato sauce

1 tablespoon oil

1 onion, chopped

1 celery stalk, chopped

2 carrots, chopped

850 g (1 lb 14 oz) tinned crushed tomatoes

1 teaspoon sugar

potato gnocchi

1 kg (2 lb 4 oz) all-purpose potatoes

30 g (1 oz) butter

250 g (9 oz/2 cups) plain (all purpose) flour

2 eggs, beaten

1 To make the tomato sauce, heat the oil in a saucepan, add the onion, celery and carrot and cook for about 5 minutes, stirring. Add the tomatoes and sugar and season. Bring to the boil, then reduce the heat to very low and simmer for 20 minutes. Cool a little, then process, in batches, in a food processor until smooth.

2 To make the potato gnocchi, peel the potatoes, chop roughly and boil until very tender. Drain and mash until smooth. Using a wooden spoon, stir in the butter and flour, then beat in the eggs. Leave to cool.

3 Turn the gnocchi mixture out onto a floured surface and divide into four. Roll each into a sausage shape.

4 Cut into short pieces and press each piece with the back of a fork. Cook the gnocchi in batches in a large saucepan of boiling salted water for about 2 minutes, or until they rise to the surface. Using a slotted spoon, drain the gnocchi and transfer to bowls. Serve with the tomato sauce.

san choy bau

SERVES 4

3 tablespoons oyster sauce

2 teaspoons soy sauce

3 tablespoons sherry

1 teaspoon sugar

1½ tablespoons vegetable oil

¼ teaspoon sesame oil

3 garlic cloves, crushed

3 teaspoons grated fresh ginger

6 spring onions (scallions), sliced on the diagonal

500 g (1 lb 2 oz) ground (minced) pork

100 g (3½ oz) bamboo shoots, finely chopped

100 g (3½ oz) water chestnuts, drained and finely chopped

1 tablespoon pine nuts, toasted

12 small or 4 large whole lettuce leaves (such as iceberg)

oyster sauce, to serve

1. To make the sauce, combine the oyster and soy sauces, sherry and sugar in a small bowl and stir until the sugar dissolves.

2. Heat a wok over high heat, add the vegetable and sesame oils and swirl to coat the wok. Add the garlic, ginger and half the spring onion and stir-fry for 1 minute. Add the pork and cook for 3–4 minutes, or until just cooked, breaking up any lumps.

3. Add the bamboo shoots, water chestnuts and remaining spring onion, then pour in the sauce. Cook for 2–3 minutes, or until the liquid thickens a little. Stir in the pine nuts.

4. Trim the lettuce leaves into cup shapes. Divide the filling among the lettuce cups to make either 12 small portions or four very large ones. Drizzle with oyster sauce, then serve.

pork, pumpkin and cashew stir-fry

SERVES 4

2–3 tablespoons vegetable oil

80 g (2¾ oz/½ cup) cashews

750 g (1 lb 10 oz) pork loin fillet

500 g (1 lb 2 oz) pumpkin (squash), cut into cubes

1 tablespoon grated fresh ginger

4 tablespoons chicken stock

3 tablespoons dry sherry

1½ tablespoons soy sauce

½ teaspoon cornflour (cornstarch)

300 g (10½ oz) bok choy (pak choy)

1–2 tablespoons coriander (cilantro) leaves

1 Heat a wok over high heat, add 1 tablespoon of the oil and swirl to coat the wok. Stir-fry the cashews for 1–2 minutes, or until browned. Remove and drain on paper towel.

2 Slice the pork thinly across the grain. Reheat the wok, add a little extra oil and swirl to coat. Stir-fry the pork in batches for 5 minutes, or until lightly browned. Remove. Add 1 tablespoon of oil and stir-fry the pumpkin and ginger for 3 minutes, or until lightly browned. Add the stock, sherry and soy sauce, and simmer for 3 minutes, or until the pumpkin is tender.

3 Blend the cornflour with 1 teaspoon of water, add to the wok and stir until the mixture boils and thickens. Return the pork and cashews to the wok, and add the bok choy and coriander. Stir until the bok choy has just wilted. Serve with steamed rice.

tofu with greens and noodles

SERVES 4

marinade

3 tablespoons oyster sauce

3 tablespoons hoisin sauce

2 tablespoons soy sauce

1½ tablespoons soft brown sugar

3 teaspoons grated fresh ginger

3 garlic cloves, crushed

300 g (10½ oz) firm tofu, drained and cut into small cubes

300 g (10½ oz) dried thin egg noodles

1 teaspoon canola oil

4 red Asian shallots, thinly sliced

1 small red capsicum (pepper), seeded and thinly sliced

200 g (7 oz) sugar snap peas, trimmed

400 g (14 oz) broccoli, cut into 5 cm (2 inch) lengths

125 ml (4 fl oz/½ cup) vegetable stock or water

1 Combine the marinade ingredients in a non-metallic bowl. Add the tofu and gently stir through. Cover and refrigerate for at least 30 minutes.

2 Cook the noodles according to the directions and drain. Cut the noodles into short lengths with scissors.

3 Heat the oil in a large wok. Add the shallots and capsicum and stir-fry for 2 minutes, or until slightly softened. Add the peas, broccoli and stock. Cover and cook for 2–3 minutes, or until the vegetables are just tender, stirring occasionally.

4 Add the tofu with the marinade and the noodles. Gently combine and stir until heated through. Serve immediately.

orange and ginger chicken stir-fry

SERVES 4–6

3 tablespoons vegetable oil

4–6 boneless, skinless chicken thighs, cut into small pieces

3 teaspoons grated fresh ginger

1 teaspoon grated orange zest

125 ml (4 fl oz/$\frac{1}{2}$ cup) chicken stock

2 teaspoons honey

550 g (1 lb 4 oz) bok choy (pak choy), trimmed and halved lengthways

toasted sesame seeds, to serve

steamed white rice, to serve

1. Heat a wok over high heat, add the oil and swirl to coat the side of the wok. Add the chicken in batches and stir-fry each batch for 3–4 minutes, or until golden.

2. Return all the chicken to the wok, add the ginger and orange zest and cook for 20 seconds, or until fragrant.

3. Add the stock and the honey and stir to combine. Increase the heat and cook for 3–4 minutes, or until the sauce has thickened slightly.

4. Add the bok choy and cook until slightly wilted. Season well, then sprinkle with toasted sesame seeds and serve with steamed rice.

sweet chilli chicken and noodles

SERVES 4

375 g (13 oz) hokkien (egg) noodles

4 boneless, skinless chicken thighs, cut into small pieces

1–2 tablespoons sweet chilli sauce

2 teaspoons fish sauce

1 tablespoon vegetable oil

100 g (3½ oz) baby sweet corn, halved lengthways

150 g (5½ oz) snow peas (mangetout), topped and tailed

1 tablespoon lime juice

1 Put the noodles in a large bowl, cover with boiling water for 1 minute, then gently separate. Drain and rinse.

2 Combine the chicken, sweet chilli sauce and fish sauce in a bowl.

3 Heat a wok over high heat, add the oil and swirl to coat the side of the wok. Add the chicken and stir-fry for 3–5 minutes, or until cooked through. Add the corn and snow peas and stir-fry for 2 minutes. Stir in the noodles and lime juice, then serve.

pork and chive dumplings

MAKES 24

1 teaspoon vegetable oil

2 garlic cloves, crushed

1 teaspoon finely grated fresh ginger

2 teaspoons snipped chives

½ carrot, finely diced

200 g (7 oz) minced (ground) pork

2 tablespoons oyster sauce

3 teaspoons salt-reduced soy sauce, plus extra to serve

½ teaspoon sesame oil

1 teaspoon cornflour (cornstarch)

24 round gow gee wrappers

1 Heat a wok over high heat, add the vegetable oil and swirl to coat the side of the wok. Add the garlic, ginger, chives and carrot, then stir-fry for 2 minutes. Remove the wok from the heat.

2 Put the pork, oyster sauce, soy sauce, sesame oil and cornflour in a bowl and mix well. Add the vegetable mixture once it has cooled, mixing it into the pork mixture.

3 Put 2 teaspoons of the mixture in the centre of each gow gee wrapper. Moisten the edges with water, then fold in half to form a semicircle. Pinch the edges together to form a ruffled edge.

4 Line a double bamboo steamer with baking paper. Put half the dumplings in a single layer in each steamer basket. Cover and steam over a wok of simmering water for 12 minutes, or until cooked through. Serve with soy sauce.

fried rice

SERVES 4

2 tablespoons peanut oil

2 eggs, well beaten

4 bacon slices, chopped

2 teaspoons finely grated fresh ginger

1 garlic clove, crushed

6 spring onions (scallions), finely chopped

50 g (1¾ oz) red capsicum (pepper), seeded and diced

1 teaspoon sesame oil

750 g (1 lb 10 oz/4 cups) cold, cooked long-grain white rice

100 g (3½ oz/⅔ cup) frozen peas, thawed

100 g (3½ oz) cooked chicken, chopped

2 tablespoons soy sauce

1 Heat a large heavy-based wok until very hot. Add about 2 teaspoons of the peanut oil and swirl to coat the wok. Pour in the eggs and swirl to coat a little up the side of the wok. Cook until just set into an omelette. Remove from the wok, roll up and set aside.

2 Add the remaining peanut oil to the wok and stir-fry the bacon for 2 minutes. Add the ginger, garlic, spring onion and capsicum and stir-fry for 2 minutes.

3 Add the sesame oil and the rice. Stir-fry, tossing regularly, until the rice is heated through.

4 Cut the omelette into thin strips and add to the wok with the peas and the chicken. Cover and steam for 1 minute, or until heated through. Stir in the soy sauce and serve.

fishcakes

SERVES 4

700 g (1 lb 9 oz) all-purpose potatoes, peeled and quartered

2 tablespoons canola oil

500 g (1 lb 2 oz) boneless white fish fillets

1 leek, white part only, finely chopped

2 garlic cloves, crushed

30 g (1 oz) chopped spring onions (scallions)

lemon wedges, to serve

1. Put the potato in a saucepan. Cover with cold water and bring to the boil. Boil for 15 minutes, or until the potato is tender. Drain well. Mash with a fork.

2. Meanwhile, heat 2 teaspoons of the oil in a large non-stick frying pan over medium heat. Add the fish fillets and cook for 3–4 minutes on each side, or until cooked. Set aside to cool. Flake the fish with a fork.

3. Heat another 2 teaspoons of the oil in the same frying pan over medium heat. Cook the leek and garlic, stirring often, for 5–6 minutes, or until the leek softens. Set aside on a plate.

4. Mix together the mashed potato, flaked fish, leek mixture and spring onion in a large bowl. Shape into eight cakes and put on a plate. Cover and refrigerate for 1 hour.

5. Heat the remaining oil in the frying pan over medium heat. Cook the fish cakes for 3–4 minutes on each side, or until lightly golden.

beer-battered fish and wedges

SERVES 4

3 all-purpose potatoes

oil, for deep-frying

125 g (4½ oz/1 cup) self-raising flour

1 egg, beaten

185 ml (6 fl oz/¾ cup) beer

4 boneless white fish fillets

plain (all-purpose) flour, for dusting

125 g (4½ oz/½ cup) tartare sauce, or mayonnaise mixed with 1 tablespoon lemon juice

1 Wash the potatoes, but do not peel. Cut into thick wedges, then dry with paper towels. Fill a heavy-based saucepan two-thirds full with oil and heat. Gently lower the potato wedges into medium–hot oil. Cook for 4 minutes, or until tender and lightly browned. Carefully remove the wedges from the oil with a slotted spoon and drain on paper towels.

2 Sift the self-raising flour with some pepper into a large bowl and make a well in the centre. Add the egg and beer. Using a wooden spoon, stir until just combined and smooth. Dust the fish fillets in the plain flour, shaking off the excess. Add the fish fillets one at a time to the batter and toss until well coated. Remove the fish from the batter, draining off the excess batter.

3 Working with one piece of fish at a time, gently lower it into the medium–hot oil. Cook for 2 minutes, or until golden and crisp and cooked through. Carefully remove from the oil with a slotted spoon. Drain on paper towels, and keep warm while you cook the remainder.

4 Return the potato wedges to the medium–hot oil. Cook for another 2 minutes, or until golden brown and crisp. Remove from the oil with a slotted spoon and drain on paper towels. Serve the wedges immediately with the fish, and tartare sauce or lemon mayonnaise.

Note: This recipe has ingredients that are deep-fried, so you'll need an adult to help you if you are cooking on your own.

burger with the works

SERVES 4

burgers

500 g (1 lb 2 oz) lean minced (ground) beef

1 onion, finely chopped

1 egg, lightly beaten

25 g (1 oz/⅓ cup) fresh breadcrumbs

2 tablespoons tomato sauce (ketchup)

2 teaspoons Worcestershire sauce

toppings

30 g (1 oz) butter

2 large onions, cut into rings

4 cheddar cheese slices

4 bacon slices

4 eggs

4 large hamburger buns, halved

1 handful lettuce leaves

1 large tomato, sliced

4 pineapple rings

tomato sauce (ketchup), to serve

1. Place all the burger ingredients in a mixing bowl. Use your hands to mix together until well combined.

2. Divide the mixture into 4 portions and shape each portion into a patty.

3. Melt the butter in a frying pan and cook the onion until soft. Set aside and keep warm.

4. Cook the burgers in the frying pan for 4 minutes each side. Place a slice of cheese on each burger, to melt.

5. Cook the bacon in the frying pan (without any butter) until crisp, then fry the eggs.

6. Toast the buns under a hot grill (broiler) for 3–5 minutes and place the bases on serving plates. On each base, place the lettuce, tomato and pineapple, then a burger. Follow with bacon, onion, egg, tomato sauce and finally the bun top.

sausage pie

SERVES 4

3 thick or 6 thin sausages

4 sheets frozen puff pastry, thawed

4 eggs

1　Put the sausages in a large bowl and cover with boiling water. Leave until cool. When cool, carefully peel the skins from the sausages and slice.

2　Use half the pastry to line a 25 cm (10 inch) pie dish or four individual dishes. Arrange the sausages evenly in the dish. Beat the eggs and season with salt and pepper, then gently pour over the sausages.

3　Preheat the oven to 190°C (375°F/Gas 5). Use the rest of the pastry to make a lid for the pie, trim the excess and seal the edges well. Cut two small slits in the middle. Cut out star shapes and place on top, if desired. Brush with some beaten egg.

4　Bake for 45 minutes. Serve hot or cold.

cactus juice

1/2 Lebanese (short) cucumber, sliced

1 litre (35 fl oz/4 cups) apple juice

1 tablespoon honey

500 ml (17 fl oz/2 cups) chilled lemonade

500 ml (17 fl oz/2 cups) soda water

1   Place the cucumber in a large bowl with the apple juice and honey. Stir to combine. Cover and refrigerate for at least 1 hour.

2   Pour into eight glasses and add the lemonade and soda water. Top with ice cubes.

foaming craters

SERVES 8

250 g (9 oz) strawberries

8 scoops vanilla ice cream

lemonade, to serve

1   In a blender or food processor, process the strawberries until smooth.

2   Divide purée evenly among eight tall glasses.

3   Place a scoop of vanilla ice cream in each glass and top with lemonade, being careful not to overfill the glass. Serve immediately.

jungle juice

SERVES 8

850 ml (29 fl oz) unsweetened pineapple juice

750 ml (26 fl oz/3 cups) apple juice

450 g (1 lb) tinned unsweetened crushed pineapple

750 ml (26 fl oz/3 cups) chilled lemonade or dry ginger ale

glacé cherries, to garnish

1   Combine the pineapple juice, apple juice and crushed pineapple in a large bowl. Stir to combine. Cover and refrigerate for at least 1 hour.

2   Pour into eight glasses and add the lemonade or dry ginger ale. Garnish with cherries.

fruit punch

SERVES 10

125 ml (4 fl oz/1/2 cup) orange juice

425 g (15 oz) tinned fruit salad

juice of 1 orange

juice of 1 lemon

750 ml (26 fl oz/3 cups) chilled lemonade

fresh fruit, such as raspberries, blueberries, apple, orange, rockmelon and honeydew melon, to garnish

1   Combine the orange juice, fruit salad and the fresh orange and lemon juices in a bowl.

2   Stir lightly to combine. Cover and refrigerate for at least 1 hour.

3   Just before serving, add the lemonade. Garnish with fresh fruit.

something
sweet

crazy cupcakes

MAKES 12

250 g (9 oz/2 cups) self-raising flour

165 g (5³/₄ oz/³/₄ cup) sugar

125 g (4¹/₂ oz) unsalted butter, softened

3 eggs

3 tablespoons milk

¹/₂ teaspoon vanilla extract

icing (frosting)

125 g (4¹/₂ oz) unsalted butter

250 g (9 oz/2 cups) icing (confectioners') sugar

2 tablespoons milk

assorted food colouring

sprinkles, to decorate (if you like)

1   Preheat the oven to 180°C (350°F/Gas 4). Line 12 standard muffin holes with paper patty cases.

2   Sift the flour and sugar into a bowl. Add the butter, eggs, milk and vanilla and beat until smooth. Fill the patty cases three-quarters full with the mixture.

3   Bake for 15 minutes, or until lightly golden. Cool on a wire rack.

4   To make the icing, beat the butter in a small mixing bowl using electric beaters until light and fluffy. Add the sifted icing sugar and milk and beat until smooth.

5   Divide the icing into three or four portions depending on how many colours you want to use. Tint portions of the icing in different colours.

6   Fill a piping (icing) bag fitted with a large star tube with the icing and pipe swirls on the cupcakes. Decorate with sprinkles if you like.

traffic light biscuits

MAKES 15

125 g (4¹/₂ oz) unsalted butter, cubed and softened

125 g (4¹/₂ oz/¹/₂ cup) caster (superfine) sugar

¹/₂ teaspoon vanilla extract

185 g (6¹/₂ oz/1¹/₂ cups) plain (all-purpose) flour

60 g (2¹/₄ oz/¹/₂ cup) custard powder

30 ml (1 fl oz) milk

1 tablespoon strawberry jam

2 tablespoons apricot jam

green food colouring

1 Preheat the oven to 200°C (400°F/Gas 6). Line a baking tray with baking paper.

2 Beat the butter and caster sugar until light and creamy. Add the vanilla and beat until combined.

3 Sift the flour and custard powder into the butter mixture. Add the milk and using a flat-bladed or palette knife, mix the ingredients together to form a soft dough. Turn out onto a lightly floured surface.

4 Roll the dough out to a neat rectangle 21 x 40 cm (8¹/₂ x 16 inches). Using a ruler as a guide, cut out 30 rectangles, each measuring 4 x 8 cm (1¹/₄ x 3¹/₄ inches).

5 Stir the strawberry jam in a bowl until smooth. Divide the apricot jam into 2 bowls and add a few drops of green food colouring to one of the bowls. Stir both until smooth. Put a small amount of red, yellow and green jam (to resemble traffic lights) on 15 of the rectangles. Spread the jam out a little.

6 Using a plain cutter with a 2 cm (³/₄ inch) hole, cut 3 evenly spaced holes from the other 15 rectangles. Take a biscuit with the holes and sandwich on top of one of the biscuits with the jam. Press gently but firmly to show the jam coming through the holes. Repeat with the remaining rectangles and jam.

7 Place the biscuits onto the tray and bake for 15–20 minutes, or until lightly golden. Leave on the tray for 5 minutes, then cool on a wire rack.

easy sponge cake with strawberries and cream

SERVES 6

30 g (1 oz) butter, melted

60 g (2¼ oz/½ cup) plain (all-purpose) flour

60 g (2¼ oz/½ cup) cornflour (cornstarch)

2 teaspoons cream of tartar

1 teaspoon bicarbonate of soda (baking soda)

4 eggs

170 g (6 oz/¾ cup) caster (superfine) sugar

2 tablespoons hot milk

300 ml (10½ fl oz) pouring (whipping) cream

1 tablespoon icing (confectioners') sugar, plus extra to dust

2 tablespoons strawberry jam

500 g (1 lb 2 oz) strawberries, hulled and sliced in half

1. Preheat the oven to 180°C (350°F/Gas 4). Grease two 20 cm (8 inch) round cake tins with the melted butter. Line the bases with baking paper. Dust the sides of the tins with a little flour, shaking out any excess.

2. Sift the flour, cornflour, cream of tartar and bicarbonate of soda into a bowl, then repeat twice.

3. Whisk the eggs and sugar in a bowl for 5 minutes, or until pale and thick. Fold in the flour mixture and the hot milk until they are just combined. Do not overmix.

4. Divide the mixture evenly between the two tins. Bake for 18–20 minutes, or until golden. Leave in the tins for 5 minutes, then turn out onto a wire rack to cool.

5. Whip the cream and icing sugar in a bowl until fluffy. Place a sponge cake on a plate and spread with jam.

6. Top with half the cream and half of the strawberries.

7. Cover with the second sponge. Spread the remaining cream over the top and top with the remaining strawberries. Dust with icing sugar to serve.

spiced scrolls

MAKES 12

250 g (9 oz/2 cups) self-raising flour

pinch of salt

30 g (1 oz) butter, chopped

185 ml (6 fl oz/³/4 cup) milk or buttermilk

spice mixture

60 g (2¹/4 oz) butter

2 tablespoons brown sugar

1 teaspoon mixed spice

60 g (2 oz) chopped pecans

1　Preheat the oven to 210°C (415°F/Gas 6–7). Lightly grease a baking tray.

2　Sift the flour and salt into a large bowl. Add the butter and rub it in lightly using your fingertips until it looks like fine breadcrumbs.

3　Make a well in the centre. Add the milk or buttermilk. Mix to a soft dough, adding more liquid if needed. Roll out to a 25 x 40 cm (10 x 16 inch) rectangle.

4　To make the spice mixture, beat the butter, brown sugar and mixed spice in a small bowl using electric beaters until light and creamy.

5　Spread the mixture over the dough and sprinkle with the pecans. Roll up from the long side.

6　Use a sharp knife to cut into 3 cm (1¹/4 inch) slices. Lay the slices close together cut side up on the tray. Bake for 12 minutes, or until golden. Cool slightly, then serve.

neenish tarts

MAKES 12

Buttercream

60 g (2¹/₄ oz) unsalted butter

60 g (2¹/₄ oz/¹/₂ cup) icing (confectioners') sugar, sifted

1 tablespoon milk

1–2 drops natural vanilla extract

12 pre-cooked tartlet cases

2 tablespoons raspberry jam

125 g (4¹/₂ oz/1 cup) icing (confectioners') sugar, extra

1 teaspoon natural vanilla extract

3 teaspoons hot water

few drops pink food colouring

1   To make the buttercream, place the butter into a small bowl. Using electric beaters, beat on high speed for 1 minute. Add the sugar, milk and vanilla. Beat until light and creamy.

2   Place ¹/₂ teaspoon jam into each tartlet case and spread over the base. Top the jam with 2 teaspoons buttercream. Smooth the surface with the back of a teaspoon.

3   Sift the icing sugar into a small bowl. Make a well in the centre. Add the vanilla and water. Stir until the mixture is smooth. Divide the icing (frosting) into two portions. Leave one portion plain and tint the remaining portion pink.

4   Spread 1 teaspoon of plain icing over half of each tartlet and allow to set.

5   Spread 1 teaspoon of pink icing over the remaining half of each tartlet and allow to set.

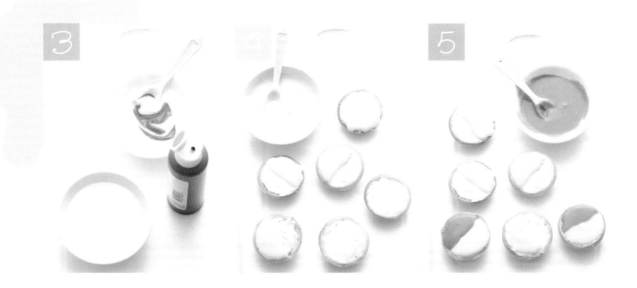

finger buns

500 g (1 lb 2 oz/4 cups) plain (all-purpose) flour

35 g (1¼ oz/⅓ cup) milk powder

1 tablespoon dried yeast

115 g (4 oz/½ cup) caster (superfine) sugar

60 g (2¼ oz/½ cup) sultanas (golden raisins)

60 g (2¼ oz) unsalted butter, melted

1 egg, lightly beaten

1 egg yolk, extra, to glaze

glace icing (frosting)

155 g (5½ oz/1¼ cups) icing (confectioners') sugar

20 g (¾ oz) unsalted butter, melted

pink food colouring

1. Mix 375 g (13 oz/3 cups) of the flour with the milk powder, yeast, sugar, sultanas and ½ teaspoon salt in a large bowl. Make a well in the centre.

2. Combine the butter, egg and 250 ml (9 fl oz/1 cup) warm water and add to the flour. Stir for 2 minutes.

3. Turn out onto a floured surface. Knead for 10 minutes, or until smooth. Place in an oiled bowl and brush with oil. Cover with plastic wrap and leave for 1 hour.

4. Grease two large baking trays. Preheat the oven to 180°C (350°F/Gas 4). Knead the dough for 1 minute. Divide into 12 pieces. Shape each into a 15 cm (6 inch) long oval. Put on the trays 5 cm (2 inches) apart. Cover with plastic wrap and set aside for 20 minutes.

5. Mix the extra egg yolk with 1½ teaspoons water and brush over the dough. Bake for 12–15 minutes, or until golden. Transfer to a wire rack to cool.

6. To make the icing (frosting), mix the icing sugar, 2–3 teaspoons water and the butter until smooth. Add the food colouring and spread over the buns.

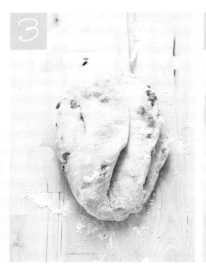

custard tarts

MAKES 12

250 g (9 oz/2 cups) plain (all-purpose) flour

60 g (2¼ oz/⅓ cup) rice flour

30 g (1 oz/¼ cup) icing (confectioners')
sugar

120 g (4¼ oz) butter

1 egg yolk

3 tablespoons iced water

1 egg white, lightly beaten

filling

3 eggs

375 ml (13 fl oz/1½ cups) milk

55 g (2 oz/¼ cup) caster (superfine) sugar

1 teaspoon vanilla extract

½ teaspoon nutmeg or ground cinnamon

1 Place the flours, icing sugar and butter in food processor. Process for 20 seconds or until crumbly. Add the egg yolk and almost all the water. Process until mixture comes together. Turn onto a lightly floured surface and press together until smooth.

2 Divide into 12 portions, roll out and line twelve 10 cm (4 inch) fluted tart tins. Refrigerate for 20 minutes.

3 Preheat the oven to 180°C (350°F/Gas 4). Cover each pastry shell with baking paper and baking beads.

4 Place on a baking tray and bake for 10 minutes. Remove from the oven and discard the baking paper and baking beads. Bake for another 10 minutes, or until golden. Brush the base and sides beaten egg white.

5 To make the filling, reduce the oven to 150°C (300°F/Gas 2). Combine the eggs and milk in a bowl and whisk. Add the sugar and vanilla and whisk. Strain the mixture, then pour into the pastry cases. Sprinkle with nutmeg and bake for 50 minutes, or until just set. Serve at room temperature.

mini berry pavlovas

MAKES 6

3 egg whites

230 g (8 oz/1 cup) caster (superfine) sugar

1 teaspoon icing (confectioners') sugar

50 g (1¾ oz) dark chocolate, melted

4 tablespoons pouring (whipping) cream

icing (confectioners') sugar, extra, to dust

½ teaspoon finely grated orange zest

assorted fresh fruit, to garnish, such as strawberries, cut into thin wedges, raspberries and blueberries, and passionfruit pulp

Preheat the oven to 150°C (300°F/Gas 2). Beat the egg whites in a large bowl until stiff peaks form. Add the icing sugar and beat until thick and very solid.

Draw twelve 7.5 cm (2½ inch) circles onto two sheets of baking paper. Turn over and place onto a baking tray.

Spread the meringue mixture over each round. Spoon the remaining meringue into a piping (icing) bag.

Pipe three circles on top of each other, leaving a small hole in the centre.

Bake for 30 minutes, or until firm to touch. Leave to cool in the oven with the door slightly ajar.

Dip the bottom of the meringue bases into the melted chocolate, then place on trays covered with baking paper and allow to set.

Whisk the cream, extra icing sugar and orange zest until just thick. Spoon into the meringues. Top with berries and passionfruit pulp.

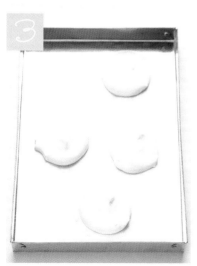

mango and passionfruit pies

MAKES 6

4 sheets ready-made puff pastry

3 ripe mangoes (900 g/2 lb), peeled and sliced or chopped, or 400 g (14 oz) tinned mango slices, drained

60 g (2¼ oz/¼ cup) passionfruit pulp, strained

1 tablespoon custard powder

90 g (3¼ oz/⅓ cup) caster (superfine) sugar

1 egg, lightly beaten

1 Preheat the oven to 190°C (375°F/Gas 5). Grease six 10 x 8 x 3 cm (4 x 3 x 1¼ inch) fluted flan tins or round pie dishes.

2 Cut out six 13 cm (5 inch) rounds from the pastry. Line the tins with the circles and trim the edges. Refrigerate until needed.

3 Combine the mango, passionfruit, custard powder and sugar in a bowl.

4 Cut out six 11 cm (4¼ inch) circles. Using any leftover pastry, cut shapes to decorate.

5 Fill the pastry cases with the mango mixture and brush the edges with egg.

6 Top with the pastry circles and press the edges to seal. Trim the edges. Decorate with the pastry shapes. Brush the tops with beaten egg.

7 Bake for 20–25 minutes, or until golden brown.

queen of puddings

SERVES 6

80 g (2³/₄ oz/1 cup) fresh white breadcrumbs

500 ml (17 fl oz/2 cups) milk, scalded

2 eggs yolks

55 g (2 oz/¹/₄ cup) sugar

3 tablespoons strawberry jam

150 g (5¹/₂ oz) strawberries, sliced

meringue

110 g (3³/₄ oz/¹/₂ cup) caster (superfine) sugar

4 egg whites

1. Preheat the oven to 180°C (350°F/Gas 4). Put the breadcrumbs in a bowl with the hot milk and leave for 10 minutes.

2. Beat the egg yolks with half the sugar and stir into the crumb mixture.

3. Spoon the mixture into a greased 900 ml (30 fl oz) ovenproof bowl and bake for 45 minutes, or until firm. Reduce the oven to warm 160°C (315°F/Gas 2–3).

4. Combine the jam and sliced strawberries and spread over the pudding.

5. To make the meringue, whisk the egg whites until stiff, then beat in the sugar. Swirl over the top of the pudding.

6. Bake for 8–10 minutes, or until the meringue is set and lightly browned. Serve hot or warm.

chocolate roll

SERVES 6–8

3 eggs

125 g (4½ oz/½ cup) caster (superfine) sugar

30 g (1 oz/¼ cup) plain (all-purpose) flour

2 tablespoons cocoa powder

250 ml (9 fl oz/1 cup) pouring (whipping) cream

1 tablespoon icing (confectioners') sugar

½ teaspoon vanilla extract

icing (confectioners') sugar, extra, to dust

1 Preheat the oven to 200°C (400°F/Gas 6). Grease a 25 x 30 cm (10 x 12 inch) Swiss roll tin (jelly roll tin). Line with paper and grease the paper.

2 Beat the eggs and 90 g (3 oz/⅓ cup) of the caster sugar in a bowl using electric beaters until thick.

3 Sift the flour and cocoa together and fold into the egg mixture. Spread into the tin. Bake for 12 minutes.

4 Place a tea towel on a work surface, cover with baking paper and sprinkle with the caster sugar. Turn the cake out onto the paper. Trim the edges.

5 Roll the cake up from the long side, rolling the paper inside the roll. Leave on a wire rack for 5 minutes, then unroll and cool.

6 Beat the cream, icing sugar and vanilla until stiff peaks form. Spread over the cake.

7 Roll the cake up again. Place the cake, seam-side-down, on a tray. Refrigerate for 30 minutes. Dust with icing sugar, then cut into slices to serve.

marble cake

SERVES 8–10

25 g (1 oz) unsalted butter

115 g (4 oz/¹/₂ cup) caster (superfine) sugar

2 eggs

¹/₂ teaspoon vanilla extract

250 g (9 oz/2 cups) self-raising flour, sifted

125 ml (4 fl oz/¹/₂ cup) milk

2 tablespoons unsweetened cocoa

¹/₈ teaspoon bicarbonate of soda (baking soda)

1 tablespoon milk, extra

few drops pink food colouring

icing (frosting)

125 g (4¹/₂ oz/1 cup) icing (confectioners') sugar, sifted

15 g (¹/₂ oz) unsalted butter, softened

¹/₂ teaspoon vanilla extract

few drops red food colouring, extra

1. Preheat the oven to 180°C (350°F/Gas 4). Grease and flour a 9 x 23 cm (3¹/₂ x 9 inch) loaf (bar) tin.

2. Cream the butter and sugar together until light and fluffy. Add the eggs one at a time, beating well. Mix in vanilla. Fold in flour alternately with milk.

3. Divide the mixture into 3 separate bowls. Add the cocoa, soda and milk to one. Leave one plain. Stir food colouring into the remaining bowl.

4. Drop alternate colours into the tin.

5. Draw a skewer or knife through the mixture in circles to streak the colours. Bake for 40–45 minutes, or until a skewer poked in the middle comes out clean.

6. Cool in the tin for 5 minutes, then turn out onto a wire rack to cool completely.

7. To make the icing, beat the ingredients and add 1–2 tablespoons of water. Spread over the top of cake.

ice cream brownie sandwiches

SERVES 6

1 litre (35 fl oz/4 cups) vanilla ice cream, slightly softened

125 g (4½ oz) unsalted butter, chopped

185 g (6½ oz) dark chocolate, chopped

250 g (9 oz/1 cup) caster (superfine) sugar

2 eggs, lightly beaten

125 g (4½ oz/1 cup) plain (all-purpose) flour, sifted

60 g (2¼ oz/½ cup) chopped walnuts or hazelnuts

unsweetened cocoa, to dust

1. Preheat the oven to 180°C (350°F/Gas 4). Line a baking tray with baking paper.

2. Spread out the ice cream to form a 15 x 20 cm (6 x 8 inch) rectangle. Cover the surface with baking paper and re-freeze it.

3. Lightly grease a 20 x 30 cm (8 x 12 inch) baking tin and line the base with baking paper, leaving a little hanging over the two longer sides.

4. Put the butter and chocolate in a heatproof bowl and set over a saucepan of simmering water. Stir the chocolate until melted. Remove and cool slightly.

5. Whisk in the sugar and eggs, then add the flour and walnuts. Stir well, then spoon into the tin.

6. Bake for 40 minutes, or until firm. Cool in the tin.

7. Cut the brownie into 12 portions and the ice cream into six.

8. Sandwich the ice cream between two pieces of brownie and dust with cocoa.

pancakes

MAKES ABOUT 12

125 g (4¹/₂ oz/1 cup) plain (all-purpose) flour

sprinkle of salt

1 egg

310 ml (10³/₄ fl oz/1¹/₄ cups) milk

lemon juice and sugar, to sprinkle

cream or ice cream, to serve

1 Sift the flour and salt into a mixing bowl and make a well in the centre.

2 Add the egg and milk. Whisk until smooth. Set aside for 1 hour.

3 Gently heat a lightly greased 20 cm (8 inch) frying pan. Pour about 3 tablespoons of batter into the pan. Tilt the pan to spread the batter evenly.

4 Lift the edges with a knife. When golden, flip the pancake over and cook the other side.

5 Sprinkle lemon juice and sugar over the pancake. Roll up and serve hot with whipped cream or ice cream, if desired.

baby choc éclairs

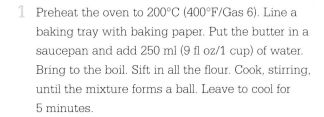

MAKES ABOUT 24

75 g (2½ oz) unsalted butter

125 g (4½ oz/1 cup) plain (all-purpose) flour

4 eggs

125 g (4½ oz) dark chocolate, melted

whipped cream, to serve

1 Preheat the oven to 200°C (400°F/Gas 6). Line a baking tray with baking paper. Put the butter in a saucepan and add 250 ml (9 fl oz/1 cup) of water. Bring to the boil. Sift in all the flour. Cook, stirring, until the mixture forms a ball. Leave to cool for 5 minutes.

2 Add the eggs, one at a time, beating well until thick and glossy. Spoon into a piping bag and pipe short lengths onto the baking tray. Sprinkle with a little water.

3 Bake for 10–15 minutes. Reduce the oven to 180°C (350°F/Gas 4) and bake for a further 10–15 minutes, or until golden and firm.

4 Pierce the side of each éclair with a skewer to allow steam to escape. Turn off the oven and return the eclairs to the oven for about 5 minutes to dry out. Cool on a wire rack.

5 Split the éclairs in half lengthways and remove any uncooked pastry. Spread the tops with chocolate, leave to set, fill with cream and replace the tops.

lemon cheesecakes

MAKES 12

250 g (9 oz) honey snap or granita biscuits

1½ teaspoons mixed (pumpkin pie) spice

125 g (4½ oz) unsalted butter, melted

filling

375 g (13 oz) cream cheese

1 tablespoon grated lemon zest

2 teaspoons vanilla extract

400 g (14 oz) tinned sweetened condensed milk

4 tablespoons lemon juice

1 Grease 12 standard muffin holes with melted butter or oil. Line each hole with two strips of baking paper.

2 Put the biscuits in a food processor and process until finely crushed. Add the spice and melted butter and process to combine.

3 Press half the crumb mixture into the bases of the muffin holes. Press the remainder around the sides of the holes. Use a flat-bottomed glass to press the crumbs firmly into place. Put in the fridge.

4 To make the filling, beat the cream cheese with electric beaters until smooth and creamy. Add the lemon zest and vanilla extract. Mix well. Gradually beat in the condensed milk and lemon juice. Beat for 5 minutes, or until the mixture is smooth.

5 Pour the filling into the crumb cases and smooth the tops. Refrigerate the cheesecakes overnight. Lift out of the muffin holes, using the baking paper handles.

flourless chocolate cakes

MAKES 8

250 g (9 oz) dark chocolate, chopped

100 g (3½ oz) caster (superfine) sugar

100 g (3½ oz) unsalted butter, cubed

125 g (4½ oz) ground hazelnuts

5 eggs, separated

icing (confectioners') sugar, to dust

1 Preheat the oven to 180°C (350°F/Gas 4). Grease eight 125 ml (4 fl oz/½ cup) mini flower-shaped tins and line the bases with baking paper.

2 Place the chocolate, sugar and butter in a heatproof bowl. Sit the bowl over a saucepan of simmering water, making sure the base of the bowl does not touch the water. Stir occasionally. Remove from the heat and stir well.

3 Transfer the chocolate mixture to a large bowl. Stir in the hazelnuts, then beat in the egg yolks, one at a time, mixing well after each addition.

4 In a separate bowl, whisk the egg whites until stiff peaks form. Gently fold into the chocolate using a metal spoon or spatula. Pour the mixture into the tin

5 Bake for 30–40 minutes, or until a skewer inserted into the centre of the cake comes out clean. Leave to cool completely in the tin, then turn out and dust with icing sugar.

jam pudding

SERVES 6

160 g (5³/₄ oz/¹/₂ cup) strawberry jam

60 g (2¹/₄ oz) unsalted butter

115 g (4 oz/¹/₂ cup) caster (superfine) sugar

1 egg

225 g (8 oz/1³/₄ cups) plain (all-purpose) flour

1 teaspoon baking powder

125 ml (4 fl oz/¹/₂ cup) milk

1   Grease six individual pudding bowls or a 1 litre (35 fl oz/4 cup) pudding bowl with butter. Spread the jam in the base.

2   Beat the butter, sugar and egg until smooth and creamy. Sift in the flour and baking powder. Add the milk and mix well. Spread the batter carefully on top of the jam in the pudding bowls.

3   Make a foil lid for each bowl. Press around the edges to seal tight. Make string handles for the bowls.

4   Put the pudding bowls into a large pan. Pour enough hot water into the pan to come a third of the way up the bowls. Put the lid on the pan and place over low heat. Simmer for 1 hour. Keep refilling with water.

5   Run a knife around the edge of each pudding. Tip onto a serving plate. Serve.

caramel sauce

SERVES 6–8

100 g (3¹/₂ oz) unsalted butter

185 g (6¹/₂ oz/1 cup) soft brown sugar

125 ml (4 fl oz/¹/₂ cup) cream

1. Combine all the ingredients in a small saucepan. Stir over medium heat until the mixture is smooth. Bring to the boil, reduce the heat slightly and simmer for 2 minutes.

strawberry sauce

SERVES 8

250 g (9 oz) strawberries

2 tablespoons caster (superfine) sugar

1 tablespoon orange or lemon juice

1. Put the strawberries, sugar and juice into a blender and blend until the mixture is smooth. Chill in the refrigerator.

hot choc sauce

SERVES 6–8

250 g (9 oz) dark chocolate

170 ml (5¹/₂ fl oz/²/₃ cup) cream

2 tablespoons golden syrup or honey

40 g (1¹/₂ oz) unsalted butter

1. Chop the chocolate roughly. Place the chocolate, cream, syrup and butter in a saucepan. Stir over low heat until the chocolate has melted and the mixture is smooth. Serve immediately.

banana split

SERVES 4

4 large ripe bananas, halved lengthways

8 small scoops vanilla ice cream

sauce of your choice

mixed lollies, to decorate

12 small white or pink marshmallows

40 g (1¹/₂ oz/¹/₄ cup) crushed nuts

1. Arrange the two halves of each banana in a long, shallow serving dish and top with two scoops of ice cream.

2. Pour over the sauce of your choice. Decorate with the lollies, marshmallows and crushed nuts and serve immediately.

frozen fruit blocks

200 ml (7 fl oz) apple juice

2 x 140 g (5 oz) tinned fruit in natural juice

1 tablespoon fresh passionfruit pulp

1. Combine the fruits, juice and pulp in a small bowl.

2. Spoon the mixture carefully into six plastic ice-block moulds with sticks.

3. Put in the freezer and allow to set overnight. When frozen, unmould ice-blocks and serve.

Notes: Ice-block moulds are available in the supermarket and selected kitchenware shops.

Use any canned fruits, pears, peaches, apricots, pineapple, fruit salad or two fruits. If fruit pieces are large, they may need to be chopped more finely.

berry jellies

SERVES 4

85 g (3 oz) sachet raspberry-flavoured jelly crystals

250 g (9 oz) mixed frozen or fresh berries (defrosted if using frozen)

2 tablespoons sugar

200 g (7 oz) low-fat vanilla yoghurt

1. Put the jelly crystals in a bowl and pour over 250 ml (9 fl oz/1 cup) of boiling water. Stir to dissolve the crystals then add 250 ml (9 fl oz/ 1 cup) of cold water.

2. Spoon 2 tablespoons of the jelly into each of four 200 ml (7 fl oz) parfait glasses. Refrigerate until set.

3. When the berries have defrosted, strain and add any berry juices to the remaining jelly. Gently stir the sugar into the berries.

4. Divide most of the fruit over the set jelly in the parfait glasses. Pour the remaining jelly over the fruit. Refrigerate for 2 hours, or until firm.

5. Carefully spoon the yoghurt over the jellies and smooth the surface. Garnish with the leftover berries.

Note: If using fresh berries, try 3–4 different varieties such as small hulled strawberries, blueberries, raspberries and blackberries.

pear slushy

SERVES 4–6

800 g (1 lb 12 oz) tinned pear halves in syrup

1 teaspoon citric acid

1 Put the pears, their syrup and the citric acid into a blender. Blend on high for 2–3 minutes.

2 Pour into a shallow metal tin and freeze for about 1 hour, or until just frozen around the edges.

3 Scrape the ice back into the mixture with a fork. Repeat every 30 minutes until the mixture consists of even-sized ice crystals.

4 Serve immediately. Allow to soften slightly in the refrigerator before serving.

5 Pile into long cups and serve with a spoon and a straw.

watermelon slushy

SERVES 6

2 kg (4 lb 8 oz/10 cups) chopped watermelon (about 1 large watermelon)

250 g (9 oz) strawberries, hulled

2 teaspoons caster (superfine) sugar

1 Combine the watermelon, strawberries and sugar in bowl. Put the mixture in a food processor and blend until smooth.

2 Pour into a shallow metal tray. Cover with plastic wrap and freeze for 2–3 hours, or until the mixture begins to freeze.

3 Return to the blender and blend quickly to break up the ice.

4 Pour into 6 glasses, then cut the reserved watermelon into 6 small triangles and fix one onto the edge of each glass.

razzle dazzle

SERVES 2

1 lime

150g (5¹⁄₂ oz) raspberries

1 teaspoon natural vanilla extract

200g (7 oz) strawberry frozen yoghurt

1 Juice the lime in a citrus press.

2 Blend the raspberries, lime juice, vanilla and frozen yoghurt in a blender or food processor until smooth.

strawberry whirl

SERVES 2

1 small, ripe banana, chopped

90 g (3¹⁄₄ oz/¹⁄₂ cup) chopped strawberries

250 ml (9 fl oz/1 cup) milk

3 scoops ice cream

1 Put the banana, strawberries, milk and ice cream in a blender or food processor.

2 Blend on high speed for 1 minute or until the mixture is smooth.

index

Published in 2009 by Murdoch Books Pty Limited

Murdoch Books Australia
Pier 8/9
23 Hickson Road
Millers Point NSW 2000
Phone: +61 (0) 2 8220 2000
Fax: +61 (0) 2 8220 2558
www.murdochbooks.com.au

Murdoch Books UK Limited
Erico House, 6th Floor
93–99 Upper Richmond Road
Putney, London SW15 2TG
Phone: +44 (0) 20 8785 5995
Fax: +44 (0) 20 8785 5985
www.murdochbooks.co.uk

Chief Executive: Juliet Rogers
Publishing Director: Kay Scarlett

Publisher: Lynn Lewis
Design concept, art direction and design: Alex Frampton
Project Manager and Editor: Gordana Trifunovic
Production: Elizabeth Malcolm
Photography: Michele Aboud (internals); Stuart Scott (cover)
Stylist: Sarah DeNardi (internals); Louise Bickle (cover)
Cover Designer: Heather Menzies
Food preparation: Julie Ray, Simon Ruffell, Mark Core

National Library of Australia Cataloguing-in-Publication entry
Title: I want to be a chef / Murdoch Books Test Kitchen.
ISBN: 9781741967852
Notes: Includes index.
Subjects: Cooks. Cookery.
Other Authors/Contributors: Murdoch Books Test Kitchen.
Dewey number: 641.5
A catalogue reference is available for this book from the British Library

PRINTED IN CHINA. Printed in 2009

Many thanks to our models Tiani Vanderburg, Chelsea Popko and Lachlan Peknice

IMPORTANT: Those who might be at risk from the effects of salmonella poisoning (the elderly, pregnant women, young children
and those suffering from immune deficiency diseases) should consult their doctor with any concerns about eating raw eggs.

CONVERSION GUIDE: You may find cooking times vary depending on the oven you are using. For fan-forced ovens,
as a general rule, set the oven temperature to 20°C (35°F) lower than indicated in the recipe. We have used 20 ml
(4 teaspoon) tablespoon measures. If you are using a 15 ml (3 teaspoon) tablespoon, for most recipes the difference will not
be noticeable. However, for recipes using baking powder, gelatine, bicarbonate of soda (baking soda), small amounts of flour
and cornflour (cornstarch), add an extra teaspoon for each tablespoon specified.